THE WORLD OF PSYCHISM
An Authoritative Study
of Mysticism and Magic

A psychological, scientific, neurological and metaphysical analysis of the psychic arts, occult sciences and allied practices.

Books by Murry Hope
Cosmic Connections
Practical Techniques of Psychic Self-Defence
The Gaia Dialogues
The Lion People
The 9 Lives of Tyo
The Paschats and the Crystal People
The Psychology of Ritual

Murry Hope's books are available from
Thoth Publications. If you live in the U.K., and wish
to receive a catalogue, send two first class stamps and a
self-addressed envelope to:
Thoth Publications, 64 Leopold Street, Loughborough,
Leicestershire, LE11 5DN. ENGLAND
Tel. 01509 210626
Those who reside outside the U.K. please enclose
U.S. $2.00 to offest the cost of international postage.
Web Address: www.thoth.co.uk
email: enquiries@thoth.co.uk

THE WORLD OF PSYCHISM
An Authoritative Study of Mysticism and Magic

by

Murry Hope

THOTH PUBLICATIONS
Loughborough, Leicestershire.

Copyright ©2001 Murry Hope

All rights reserved. No reproduction, copy or transmission of this publication may be made without written permission. No paragraph of this publication may be reproduced, copied or transmitted save with written permission or in accordance with the provision of the Copyright Act 1956 (as amended). Any person who does any unauthorised act in relation to this publication may be liable to criminal prosecution and civil claims for damages.

The Moral Rights of the Author have been asserted.

A CIP catalogue record for this book is available from the British Library.

Cover design by Martin Jones

Printed and bound in Great Britain

Published by Thoth Publications
64, Leopold Street, Loughborough, LE11 5DN
First published 2001

ISBN 1 870450 44 2

ACKNOWLEDGEMENTS

My sincere thanks to The College of Psychic Studies, who published my Autobiography *The Changeling* (1999), for allowing me to repeat extracts from their publication which I felt might serve to illustrate to my readers, through the avenue of my personal experiences, the message I have been trying to convey throughout this book.

To Professor Peter Stewart, D.Sc.,M.Sc., for providing me with details of Dr.Barbara McClintock's amazing experience, and the experimental evidence provided by research into Remote Viewing.

And to Maria Schiller, who kindly took on the onerous task of proof-reading the ensuing pages.

I dedicate this book to all those Psychics, Mystics, Healers, Occultists and Arcane Seekers, be they scientists, physicians or lay folk, whose quest for knowledge and enlightenment is tempered by kindness, caring, generosity of spirit and a love, understanding, and acknowledgement of ALL life-forms extant throughout this and other Universes in those Timeless worlds beyond our present limited understanding.

CONTENTS

Introduction   9

CHAPTER

1. DEFINITIONS   13
   Medium, Occultist, Mystic, Shaman?: Positive/Active - Negative/Receptive: Shamanism.

2. THE MEDIUMISTIC APPROACH   22
   The Channelling Phenomenon: Development Circles: Alien Contacts: The Interpretation Factor.

3. THE DIVINATORY ARTS AND OTHER POPULAR PRETERNATURAL ACTIVITIES.   34
   The Psychic Factor: Clairvoyance: Remote Viewing: Astral Projection and The Psychic 'Bodies': Psychometry: Astrology: Palmistry: Numerology: Phrenology: Tarot and similar Divinatory Systems.

4. THE 'NEW AGE' EPISODE   46
   The Onset of Chaos: The Guru Cult: Self-Discovery and the Meditative Practices: The Butterfly Syndrome: Walk-Ins.

5. THE HEALING ARTS   55
   Healing - Vocation, Gift or 'Acquisition': The Cancer Enigma: The Counselling Craze: Therapies - Their Use and Abuse.

6. RELIGION, PSYCHISM AND THE SPIRITUALITY TRAP   57
   The Definition of 'Belief': The Psychic Factor: Wiccan, Pagan and Celtic Approaches: The Spirituality 'Trap'.

7. REINCARNATION, GENETIC MEMORY, DREAMS AND PARALLEL UNIVERSES   80
   The Karma Hypothesis: Enter the Genes: Genetic Memory: Dreams and Parallel Universes: Paschat Teachings.

8.	THE KINGDOMS OF ELEMENTALS, DEVAS AND ANGELS	91

The Four (or Five?) Elemental Forces - Eastern and Western Concepts: Devic Evolution: Angels of Time: Where does 'God' fit in?

9.	MAGIC/OCCULTISM - THE FACTS BEHIND THE FICTION	103

Different Magical Systems: Initiation - the Real Facts: The 'Lodge' System: Pathworkings: Magic and Money: The Nine Metaphysical (Cosmic) Laws: Occultism and Science: Occult Ranking Systems.

10.	RITUAL - FACTS, FANTASIES AND THE 'FEEL GOOD' FACTOR	115

The Nature and History of the Rite - A Psychological Analysis: The Sacred Instruments of Magical Ritual: Setting up a Rite: 'Black' Magic: Ritual in Contemporary Religious Practices: Secret Societies - Beware!.

11.	THE BASIC PRINCIPLES OF PSYCHIC SELF-DEFENCE	128

Is Psychic Protection Really Necessary?: The Nature of Evil: Psychic Attacks: The Effect of Drugs and Artificial Stimuli: Time Symbols.

12.	OCCULT SELF-DEFENCE	136

Curses, and how to remove them: The Mechanics of Exorcism: Beware The Power Seekers: The Dangers of Mixing Systems: The Ethics of Magic - Is Intention the Deciding Factor?

13.	THE PSYCHOLOGY OF PSYCHISM AND MAGIC	147

The Eight Psychological Types: The Introvert/Extrovert Complex - Psychological Identifications: Know Your Archetypes: The Occult side-effects of Drugs and Other Artificial Stimulants: Questionnaires for (a) Psychics; (b) Occultists.

14.	THE BRAIN - A BIOLOGICAL COMPUTER	161

Who (or What) Effects our Neural Programming?: The Neuro-Mechanisms of Religion: The Role of the Brain in the Hominid Evolutionary Plan.

Epilogue. *169*
Bibliography *171*
Recommended Reading *173*

INTRODUCTION

It is currently *de rigueur* to consult psychics, astrologers, healers, mediums, occultists, tarot readers and the many others who claim to possess knowledge of a metaphysical nature ... or talents beyond those normally associated with the five physical senses. All this, plus the many New Age fads, burgeoning Guru Cults and the rising obsession with ancient belief systems such as those of Indian, Tibetan, Egyptian, Celtic, Norse, and Amerindian origin (few of which would conform to today's standards of political correctness!) has proved a veritable 'open-sesame' not only to the genuinely gifted, but also to the ego-trippers, the self-deluded, the mentally unstable and those rogues and charlatans who masquerade under a cloak of false spirituality or self-proclaimed but totally unfounded occult prowess. With the money-bags of Mammon hovering enticingly as bait, many genuine seekers who are unfamiliar with these somewhat shady areas of metaphysical practice can be easily enticed into their web of intrigue, to the extent that not only are their bank balances adversely affected but in some cases their mental health and social well-being.

So, what guidelines are there for those trusting and oft-times gullible souls who put their faith in suspect practitioners, and how can the observers, and the purveyors of metaphysical wares themselves for that matter, assess whether the information being dispensed is genuinely inspired from exalted dimensions/well intentioned communicators, or purely self-delusion?

Over my seventy-one years - some fifty-six of which have been involved in metaphysical studies - I have encountered plenty of fakes, inadequates and those beguiled into the belief that they possess psychic or occult powers. Modern advertising hypes frequently bill such people as 'The Greatest Healer in the U.K.', 'America's

Favourite Psychic', 'The Amazing Master from Tibet', and so forth. I do not need to emphasise how many unsuspecting members of the public are impressed by such nonsense. Huge fees are frequently charged for the dubious privileges of the 'services' on offer by such people, either as speakers or for private consultation. The Labourer may well be 'worthy of his or her hire', but only if his/her gifts are genuine and not engendered by fakery, self-delusion or ego-tripping. Metaphysical skills, and the wisdom to use them safely and compassionately, cannot be equated with university degree-like qualifications which guarantee one results if the answers given are acceptable to the examiners; nor can they be bought. One has to evolve into them.

The fact to be faced, however, is that there are still many who are at a stage in their psychological development which precludes them from pursuing the lone path and working things out for themselves. Either they feel safe within those creeds or cults which offer them numerical support, or they have a psychological need to 'follow', be that an organised religion or a questionable guru. From a psychological standpoint all this is perfectly understandable. Like it or not, the cloak of orthodoxy does, to a certain extent, offer a comfortable umbrella under which to shelter from the so-termed 'evils' to be encountered along the path of self-seeking or individuation.

However, with the rapidly increasing metamorphosis in the cosmic frequencies around this planet, and in our solar system generally, the climate of belief is also undergoing a radical transmutation too rapidly, it would seem, for some. The worst nightmares of those who have abandoned regular Church-going for more modern scenarios are no longer clothed in visions of hell and damnation, but in strange aliens who abduct people for dubious experimental purposes, or Godzilla-like creatures large enough to invade our space unless checked by our noble scientists in cohorts with the great military machine. In simple language, our 'devils' have changed contours and 'hell' has acquired a cosmic flavour. Into that newly-engendered vacuum which our changing world has created, have stepped those earlier mentioned psychic-cum-spiritual practitioners who have been standing in the proverbial 'wings', ready and waiting to assume their somewhat questionable roles in the drama of these rapidly changing times. Fortunately there are those who have refused to become caught up in this pseudo-cosmic media hype, while also electing to forgo orthodoxy, by-pass the gurus and opt for the metaphysical approach, either via the lone path, small group or 'Lodge' situation. However, contrary to what some might think, this is not as simple as reading a book, seeing the movie and getting the tee-shirt or, in practical terms, consulting the local medium, getting a good tarot reading or joining some ancient Egyptian, Amerindian, Shamanic or Druidic Order that has updated to accommodate the modern psyche. Let us look at it this way; how many of us would rush across a busy thoroughfare without first looking right, left and right again, to check for oncoming traffic or other obstacles that might be likely to impede our progress? Yet it would seem that otherwise sane and stable people will happily plunge headlong into unknown dimensions or uncharted areas of consciousness without observing even the simplest precautions.

This naturally gives rise to the question 'What is there to be afraid of and why should we need to protect ourselves'? Fair comment. Well, first of all, as the old saying goes, 'to know your enemy is half the battle', and few people really know what they are letting themselves in for when they embark on a course which, in some cases anyway, denies the use of reason. There are, in fact, many levels of consciousness and even more parallel universes, into which we may accidentally stumble. Those unfortunates who enter such realms without prior knowledge as to how to extract themselves can end up on the psychiatrist's couch, or worse!

To confuse the matter even further, a newcomer has entered this bizarre metaphysical scene - the human brain itself! Thankfully, neuroscience has now established that the brain is a kind of biological computer which conforms to the same behavioural patterns as its mechanical counterpart. Like the machine, it, too, has its hardware (genetic limitations), and its software - the program effected by environmental and other externally programmed sources (or self-selection, as in the case of the individuated soul). However, in order to comprehend the cerebral complexities which neuroscience appears to have established, some clear lines of demarcation are obviously called for at several levels. For example, how many of those so-termed 'revelations' are simply the product of the brain itself, and not instigated by intelligences from external sources, cosmic or otherwise?

Observations gathered from the neurological, psychological and paraphysical research are therefore required if one is to establish the real *modus operandi* involved in such practices as (a) mundane psychism, (b) remote viewing, (c) pathworkings and allied meditation techniques, (d) the uses and abuses of ritual, etc., and how such studies and practices, if approached without discipline and a modicum of precaution, can exert an adverse effect on both physical and mental health.

In the light of the aforementioned, it would be illogical to assume that anyone reading this book would fail to ask what entitles me to forward such a forceful critique? All such information is contained in my autobiography *The Changeling* (published by The College of Psychic Studies, London, in 1999). But suffice it to say that although I was born with what are viewed by some as 'paranormal' gifts, in addition to acquainting myself with the magical belief-systems of other cultures worldwide and the works of the great scientist/occultists of the past, I have, over the years, also effected an in-depth study of psychology, anthropology, the history and pre-history of this planet, quantum physics and the sciences generally, especially as related to the nature of Time. For without such knowledge I would have had no criteria against which to evaluate the accuracy (or otherwise) of inspiration, and would simply have teetered at the edge of reason, always lacking the terminology (neural software!) to express or formulate what little I have been able to discover. I am also a proponent of what is known as 'The Field Theory', a scientific hypothesis that conceives of consciousness (the soul or spirit) as being 'A field of active particles begging organisation'. Since fields of all kinds come in varying band-widths, the soul also evinces a band-width appropriate to its state of maturity - the older the soul the wider the band-width, and therefore the greater its facility for obtaining knowledge by touching onto, or connecting with, wider fields (older souls).

So, if I can pass even a modicum of this knowledge on to others then I might, and I emphasise might, have taken one small, but significant step along my own path of cosmic learning and devic understanding.

CHAPTER 1

DEFINITIONS

Medium, Occultist, Mystic, Shaman?

In this day and age the word 'psychic' seems to have acquired a multitude of different meanings for different people. Were a public survey to be carried out on the subject the answers would probably sound something like this: 'Psychics - aren't they people who foretell the future?'. 'You can knock it as much as you like but Psychic counselling certainly helped me.' 'The messages I receive from the mediums at my local Spiritualist Church have sustained me during many a dark day'. 'A load of rubbish - no scientific evidence to support it whatsoever'. 'Con artists, the lot of them'. 'Just another ploy to extract money from the gullible under false pretences'. 'Consulting with evil - the work of the Devil!'. The definition rendered by my dictionary effects a disparate approach, while also being less judgmental in describing the adjective as: '1(a) Outside the possibilities defined by natural laws, such as mental telepathy; (b) (of a person) sensitive to forces not recognised by natural laws. 2. Mental as opposed to physical - *n*. 3. A person who is sensitive to parapsychological forces or influences.'[1] In fact, modern psychology has supplied us with a mini-dictionary of words associated with matters metaphysical: preternatural, prescience, supraphysical, supramundane, PSI - one could go on.

However, like it or not, psychism and allied studies are here to stay. But has it ever been otherwise? Hardly. According to the earliest anthropological records, hominids have always acknowledged the supernatural in one form or another, usually for help to ward off natural disasters or, more often, as a means of obtaining whatever represented good fortune to the enquirer. But since there is an aspect of the Infinite in all creatures if only, perhaps, a tiny spark in younger souls, it would seem only natural that at some point along our evolutionary journey we might seek to contact that 'light' within us, either for spiritual reasons or simply to alleviate the tensions and sufferings inflicted (or self inflicted) during our sojourn on this planet we call Earth.

Not to be outdone by the past, however, modern society has created its own set of metaphysical semantics, the best known of which is probably 'channelling', (a practice which was referred to in the days of my youth as 'trance mediumship'). Due to its current popularity, however, and the tendency for many listeners to take what is said as gospel, an in-depth examination will be effected in Chapter 2, the latest studies in psychology and neuroscience suggesting alternative explanations for these phenomena.

Positive/Active - Negative/Receptive.

The whole scenario that is broadly categorized as 'psychic' actually falls into several metaphysical categories, each of which aims to effect a communication with dimensions external to the purely physical. However, it is unfortunate that certain legitimate terms sometimes carry dark connotations, the word 'occult', being an example. Any dictionary will tell you that it simply means 'hidden', its use in astronomy never seeming to give offence to anyone in the scientific or rational fields of thinking. Likewise with the word 'magic', and I could not do better than quote the words of the great Victorian metaphysical scholar Arthur Edward Waite. In his book *The Occult Sciences*, he writes:

> The popular conception of Magic, even when it is not identified with the trickeries and imposture and the pranks of the mountebank, is entirely absurd and gross.
>
> 'Magic, or, more accurately, Magism, says Christian in his 'Histoire de la Magie', if anyone would condescend to return to its antique origin, could be no longer confounded with the superstitions which calumniate its memory. Its name is derived to us from the Greek words, MAGOS, a magician, and MAGELA, Magic, which are purely permutations of the terms MOG, MEGH, MAGH, which, in Pehlvi and in Zend, both languages of the eldest East, signify "priest", "wise", and "excellent". It was

DEFINITIONS

thence also that, in a period anterior to historic Greece, there originated the Chaldean name Maghdim, which is equivalent to "supreme wisdom", or sacred philosophy. Thus, mere etymology indicates that magic was the synthesis of those sciences once possessed by the Magi or philosophers of India, of Persia, of Chaldea, and of Egypt, who were the priests of nature, the patriarchs of knowledge, the founders of those vast civilizations whose ruins still remain, without tottering, the burden of sixty centuries.

Ennemoser in his *History of Magic* (as translated by Howitt) says

> Among the Parsees, the Medes and the Egyptians, a higher knowledge of nature was understood by the term Magic, with which religion, and particularly astronomy, were associated. The initiated and their disciples were called Magicians - that is, the Wise - which was also the case among the Greeks ... Plato understood by Wisdom nothing less than a worship of the Divinity, and Apuleius says that Magus means, in the Persian language, a priest ... India, Persia, Chaldea and Egypt, were the cradles of the oldest magic. Zoroaster, Ostanes, the Brahmins, the Chaldean sages, and the Egyptian priests, were the primitive possessors of its secrets. The priestly and sacrificial functions, the healing of the sick, and the preservation of the secret wisdom, were the objects of their life. They were either princes themselves, or surrounded princes as their counsellors. Justice, truth, and the power of self-sacrifice, were the great qualities with which each one of these must be endowed; and the neglect of any one of these virtues was punished in the most cruel manner.'[2]

This erudite apology continues for several more pages, but the essence of its message is the same throughout and applies even more so to this day and age than when it was first published in 1891. However, since many of those who read this book are probably more familiar with the semantics employed among the majority of adherents to today's metaphysical beliefs, I would like to define my use of certain terms that could prove either frightening or offensive to some.

Commensurate with my present understanding, the genuine occultist (or magician), aspires to negotiate and control forces of a cosmic or paranormal nature by the use of mind-power or ritual; the psychic/medium/channeller presumes to be assisted or manipulated by essences or intelligences external to the purely physical; the mystic seeks to imbibe and merge his/her consciousness with both the manifest and unmanifest through prayer, contemplation and observation, while the Shaman seeks his or her contact with the Infinite via nature and the animal kingdoms.

However, for those among my readers whose approach to the occult arts is similar to that of the great scientists of the past, I will endeavour to effect a more scientifically acceptable description of magic/occultism:

> A body of knowledge concerned with natural cosmic laws which, due to an over-emphasis on the worlds of physical matter, has become severed from the scientific mainstream. So-called 'occult mysteries' are therefore nothing more or less than ancient scientific facts that have become encoded into terms of reference easily understood by the unlettered, many of which have, over the centuries, degenerated into superstition, their true meaning having been long since forgotten.

Magic or occult energy works at three main levels:

i) The manipulation of particle aggregates (matter/mass) via the agency of mind.
ii) The conscious negotiation of particle/wave packets in non-locality (subtle energies on the inner planes in popular esoteric parlance).
ii) Imitating certain basic universal principles or patterns which have the effect of setting corresponding events into motion at the physical level - a process referred to as 'sympathetic magic'. Of course we can always simplify the above by replacing the terminology of modern physics with appropriate elemental or angelic nomenclatures, which angle I shall be covering in a later Chapter.

In due deference to the views and researches of brighter minds than my own, perhaps I should also add to the above Rex Stanford's PMIR (Psi-mediated Instrumental Response), in which he suggests that many of us are unconsciously using magical powers to manipulate events to our advantage, hence there is no such thing as 'coincidence'. But now we are entering the world of psychology and parapsychology, which are deserving of a separate appraisal in a later Chapter.

Of course it can be argued that those practising in any of the above mentioned categories could equally be using their specific areas of expertise to contact hostile or less desirable energies, and the Universe is not, I can assure you, short of these, as anyone who has studied Angelology will know only too well.

And then there are those forms of psychic/occult expression that are exclusive to certain cultures such as Kahuna and Macumba. However, as it would take a tome to do justice to all these I shall concentrate on those that are better known. After all, it is primarily the ethics that are of interest, while the labelling of magic, for example, as 'black' or 'white' is hardly politically correct. The area in which one is trying to effect a 'difference' is that of intention, the use of mystical practices purely for self-gain or aggrandisement hardly being conducive to the attraction of more elevated beings or energies.

Arrayed against this background of diverse supraphysical studies and beliefs are conclusions arrived at by many psychiatrists, psychologists and neuroscientists - that so much so-termed 'psychic/occult' material is purely the product of the brain itself, either in its escapist mode, or due to cerebral malfunctioning of some kind.

Shamanism

There has been a recent resurgence of interest in the shamanic approach which has been aided by several factors, including the repeal of the Witchcraft Act in 1951 which allows Wiccans the freedom to practise their religion in the open, the Gaia and Green Movements, and the acknowledgment of the right of ethnic minorities to pursue their traditional beliefs without prejudice. In other words, Shamanism has suddenly become a wide umbrella under which many minor belief systems have sought shelter.

But is there such a thing as genuine or original Shamanism? Although the word 'shaman' is popularly used in connection with the North American Indian culture, where it is pronounced 'sharman', the word 'shaman' actually originated in the Ural mountains of Russia. Shamanism dates back to Cro-Magnon times and earlier, as may be evidenced in cave paintings in Europe and Aboriginal carvings in Australia. From the latter we may gather that it was probably a normal mode employed for dialogue with those gods, nature spirits or animal soul-essences which dominated both the consciousness and collective unconscious of the first hominids to grace the surface of our planet. Shamans are often referred to in the 'wounded healer' context, ancient initiatory rites having demanded both mental and physical suffering on the part of the aspirant before he/she was deemed ready to enter general practice.

Although the shaman can act as a bridge between mankind and both the subtle dimensions and the many other life-forms which inhabit this planet, shamans were not, and are not, magicians or mediums in the accepted sense of these terms, since they embrace both the yin and the yang (positive/active - as with the occultist or magician, and negative/receptive, as with the medium or psychic). In the Western Tradition it would seem that those pursuants of the metaphysical path tend to veer to one side or the other of the latter polarity, although the true occultist who has reached a certain stage (very high rank) in his/her development, can negotiate either at will. But more of that later.

Shamanistic rites are more flowing and less structured than those employed by magicians as a whole. They feel and sense the needs of the moment, as it were. Shamanism was evident in the early tribal systems of all countries. There were (and still are) Eskimo (Innuit) shamans, Siberian shamans, the many versions of shamanism encountered in North and South America, Polynesian shamans, Australian Aboriginal shamans, Celtic shamans and the shamans indigenous to our own isles who were here before the Celts arrived. However, not all 'medicine men' or those practising the psychic arts are shamans.

Since shamanism involves a strong connection with the elemental and animal kingdoms, the true shaman acknowledges the life-force, field or soul, as being present in ALL life forms, and does not limit his/her understanding of the hereafter to the hominid species. Some work with the spirits of trees, others with rocks, plants, animals, fish or reptiles. As I have covered this subject in some detail in my book *The Psychology of Ritual*, I would refer the reader to the more detailed information of a shamanic nature (rites, etc.), especially the close relationship between the Innuit shamans and their day to day life among the frozen wastes that are their homeland.

Contrary to what many New Age followers might choose to believe, shamanism does NOT rely on noise (drums, loud chanting, etc.) to effect a connection with either 'natural' dimensions (the spirits of other life forms on this planet such as plants, mountains, animals, etc.), or what are felt to be more 'exalted' dimensions. In fact, such distractions are frequently frowned upon by those shamans who aspire to a gentler and more civilised approach to their art. It has been said, and I for one agree with the statement, that only in silence can we hear the small, still voice of God - and that, surely, goes for any god, angel, or whichever term one may choose to employ to describe that All Oneness, Timeless, Infinite Mind of which we are all minute fragments.

How, why and where did these four categories, and their various offshoots, originally arise? In ancient times mediums (psychics) and magicians (occultist-priests) worked in concert, the often obscure utterances of the former being interpreted by the latter. The Old Testament of the Bible tells us that 'Zadok the Priest and Nathan the Prophet anointed Solomon King' (a statement later set to music by Handel in his famous and greatly moving Coronation Anthem).

And what more evidence for this dual practice can we have than the Delphic Oracle itself, where the Pythoness entered a state of trance and her mutterings, (which, we gather, were somewhat obscure), were interpreted for the enquirer by the attendant priests. These interpretations would often manifest as cledones, a rather distinctive form of ancient Greek psychic communication which involved 'listening' for the God's answer to one's request. Some of the Greek Oracles would answer only if consulted in a cledonistic manner. For example, certain statues - notably that of the oracle of Hermes Agoraios - were approached by the client who would cover his ears when whispering his request into the ear of the god. He would then uncover them and the first thing he heard would be taken as the God's answer to his question. The words of children were also heeded by the oracles, the belief being that they are less likely to monitor their statements than adults. (How true - monitoring, I mean!) Here is a classical example of how a cledone works, which I included in my book *The Greek Tradition*: - In his first epigram, Callimarchus describes the visit made by a client to Pittacos of Mytilene, one of the seven sages of Greece (the other six sages are Thales of Miletus, Solon of Athens, Cleobulus, Chilon, Periander and Bias) to seek advice regarding the choice of a wife. Would it be better for him to marry a girl of his own class or seek a wealthier and nobler union? The sage did little more than point to some children playing with their tops in the street and remark 'See them? They will teach you what you should do.' As he approached the group of children, the man heard one of them call out, 'Keep in line,' which he immediately understood to mean that he should abandon any ideas he had about marrying for money or rank. [3] In his book *Greek Oracles* Flaceliere comments that the famous *Tolle, Lege* of St.Augustine's *Confessions*, was uttered by a child and was a cledonistic oracle of the same kind. [4]

The point I am trying to make in all this is that the tradition of psychics (mediums) and occultists working together goes back a very long way, and there have been very few, even among the 'greats', who have managed both sides of the polarity on their own. While it is not uncommon for a 'positive' to move occasionally into the mediumistic side, the reverse is by no means a common occurrence, which tells one rather a lot about the psychological make-up of those who are more drawn to psychic receptivity.

It is often commented on how the Western mind, or way of thinking, is inclined towards a more outward approach to the paranormal, whereas the people of the East are drawn more to the mystical or meditative modes of spirituality. Although this may appear to be so on the surface, there are actually just as many practitioners of the magical and mediumistic arts in the Orient as there are in the Occident - they just use a slightly different *modus operandi*. Likewise in the West, where a heightened interest in meditation and allied studies has increased over the past few decades.

Another view of the various metaphysical approaches outlined above is that each one aligns with the nature of the four elements thus:

    FIRE   - The Occultist or Magician (who commands)
    AIR   - The Medium or channeller (who communicates)
    WATER - The Mystic (who flows and blends)
    EARTH - The Shaman (who unites with the Earth and Her creatures).

The fifth element, Time, was referred to as 'aether' in certain earlier beliefs whose adherents were not familiar with the dominating nature of this recently acknowledged source of energy. Unless Time slows down, matter cannot manifest. As Professor Stephen Hawking recently explained in his *Instanton Theory*, Time is the cosmic touchpaper that ignites the other four explosive energies which go to create the mass (matter) of which our Universe is composed (The Strong Nuclear Force - FIRE: Electromagnetism - AIR; The Weak Nuclear Force - WATER; and Gravity - EARTH). The Masters of those Timeless Worlds are often viewed in certain religious beliefs in the Angelic context; while to the Ancient Egyptians they were the Neters, and to peoples of the Indian sub-continent - the Devas.

Time exists at more frequencies than the majority of people could ever imagine. When the average hominid dies, his/her vision of the hereafter is limited by two factors - the program held by the neural software at the time of passing and the time band-width frequency, or cosmic level in which it finds itself. In simple terms, the bandwidth of Time entered by the average hominid at death is contingent upon (a) soul-age and level of understanding of the viewer, and (b) what he/she has been taught (programmed) to expect. However, the higher frequencies of Time are always open to those who have, by virtue of their deeds, understanding, bravery and cosmic comprehension, individuated from the hominid collective. And likewise those devic souls who have added Time to their already fourfold natures. In other words, no matter in which terms you may choose to couch it - there is no quick route to 'heaven'!

And while on the subject of 'heaven', in spite of scientist Carl Sagan's famous comment: 'The first priest was the first rogue who met the first fool,' the 'priestly' role, continues to dominate religious practices worldwide, Let us be optimistic, however, and hope that sooner or later the individuation process will percolate throughout the whole human race - well, what is left of it after Gaia has effected her 'cleansing' act!

In the later Chapters I shall be dealing with some of the more mundane manifestations of the negative/receptive aspect of psychism, and those tools which serve as a focus for the numerous 'readers' whose services are now available to the public at large. And, of course, the occult proper!

1   *New Collins Dictionary & Thesaurus. Collins, London & Glasgow, 1987*
2   *The Occult Sciences (Waite, A.E.). Kegan, Paul, Trench, Truber & Co.Ltd. 1891*
3   *Greek Oracles (Flaceliere, R.) Elek Books, 1965.*
4   *Ibid.*

CHAPTER 2

THE MEDIUMISTIC APPROACH

The Channelling Phenomenon

I have never considered myself so much a writer than as a dispenser of information on the one hand and 'Devil's Advocate' on the other. However, I am a fervent believer in seeing both sides of any coin. So, before I embark on the following review of the channelling scenario I would like to make one point quite clear: while I agree that we are all endowed with a degree of the psychic faculty, which may manifest through avenues such as dreams, intuition and the many areas of everyday human experience, channelling a definite message - or set of instructions - is rather a different kettle-of-fish, which the channeller who has any sense of responsibility should think about seriously. Deceptions can so easily be accomplished and the listeners 'taken in'; the deceit, or ignorance as the case may be, sometimes stemming from the communicator rather than the channeller.

This so-termed 'New Age' abounds with channellers: people who close their eyes and assume a totally different personality. As I mentioned previously, in my youth there used to be a type of channelling which was labelled 'trance mediumship', in which the medium assumed the personality of a 'guide'. Guides came in all shapes and sizes, the most popular being Red Indians. The reason given for this (by the Guides themselves) was that these intelligences were closer to the spirit world while in incarnation, which therefore gave them easier access to the minds of mortals once they had shed their physical bodies. Sometimes the messages given were simple and personal, while on other occasions the communications would

THE MEDIUMISTIC APPROACH

involve philosophical discussions, ethical disputations, or some form of spiritual teaching. Details rendered of the 'after life', 'summer lands', etc. were quite common, and the information imparted often found its way into print, to be much treasured by those who elected to follow a particular 'guide'.

So why the new name? Is there really any difference, and can anybody do it? According to a recent publication, the answer is 'yes', although I, for one am highly sceptical for the following reasons:

i) I have on more than one occasion been required to sort out the psychological problems resulting from this particular practise (and other curiosity dabblings).

ii) A lot of the so-called 'spiritual teaching' is nothing more than an emotionally charged rehash of various orthodox religious dogmas.

iii) Prophetic information rendered is often proven to be totally incorrect.

iv) It is not uncommon for these entities to contradict each other, and themselves, on occasions.

v) There are those Christians who purport to follow the teachings of their Founder, but conveniently forget the relevant passages in Matthew 24 which warn against 'false prophets' and 'false Christs'.

vi) When those 'disaster' prophecies which were supposed to have taken place late in the last millennium failed to manifest, the usual excuse was that the event foretold had been 'postponed' by 'higher powers'(?), or that mankind has been 'saved' from the aforewarned cosmic cataclysm, either by the intervention of a 'Master', or because certain groups had 'meditated' to stop it! (And by the way, why are these so-termed 'Masters' cast mostly in the masculine role?)

Taking all these points into consideration, I fail to understand why so many people are taken in by the simple fact that someone closes their eyes and claims to hand over their consciousness to another 'mind'. It is little wonder that parapsychologist Dr. Serena Roney-Dougal described channelling as 'A monologue for which nobody wishes to claim responsibility.'[1]

Over the past few years we have been treated to a series of channelled 'messages' relating to changes destined to take place on the Earth's surface, the one which springs to mind being the 'photon-belt scare'. This information, channelled in the U.S.A., warned of an approaching field of intense photon activity which would cancel out electricity worldwide, thus rendering the whole planet in a state of chaos. So convinced were the avid followers of this trash that many set up 'safe havens', which were well supplied with alternative lighting arrangements. Needless to say, the prophesied day came and went without event. When questioned as to what had gone wrong, or what god-like power had stepped in to 'save' mankind from this awful fate, the communicating entity/entities (or the mind/brain of the channeller?) came up with the usual 'postponement for good behaviour', stuff among other, more detailed excuses! (Shades of Nineveh, Jonah, and all that!) This is but one example.

I was approached by several disappointed believers at the time, who wanted more details about what had gone wrong. I suggested that in the event of a similar prophecy cropping up in the future, they ring The British Observatory at Greenwich, whose astronomers would soon be able to tell them whether there had been, or were likely to be, any astronomical phenomena of this nature. Why, oh why does logic fly out of the proverbial window when mysticism of this hyped-up variety appears on the metaphysical horizon? One supposes the cause to be the innate desire on the part of many people to experience the mystical on the one hand, or simply to escape from the responsibilities of 'thinking' on the other.

To reiterate my earlier statement, I am not disputing the fact that it is possible for the human brain to accommodate the thoughts, feelings and information contained in the data-banks of other fields (souls) either incarnate or discarnate. This has been proven many times, not only in psychic circles but also in experiments carried out by qualified parapsychologists, and in recent studies of telepathy and remote viewing, (the latter of which I shall be dealing with in a subsequent Chapter). I must also make it quite clear at this point that over my many years of working with, and observing these phenomena, I have encountered some amazingly accurate work, both in the areas of trance mediumship (no apology for the antiquated semantics) and straight clairvoyance.

THE MEDIUMISTIC APPROACH 25

So, should anyone deduce from the aforesaid that I totally disregard the idea of beings from elevated frequencies using the human brain via which to deliver their message, may I state categorically that this is NOT the case. How could any of us learn without inspiration from 'higher sources'? What I am questioning is (a) the real source of many of these channellings, (b) how much of the data given is simply the work of the brain of the channeller, there being no external entity there in the first place, and (c) how often is the information rendered simply a hotch-potch of something someone has said, or a point of ethics raised in one of the many media outlets?

So, what are the criteria against which the channeller may assess the authenticity of the channel? Is his/her neural software up to coping with, for example, genuine scientific data? And in how many cases is the channel simply another aspect of the channeller?

The photon incident mentioned above is a typical example of someone who has accidentally, perhaps, picked up a piece of cosmic information but, lacking the neural software (scientific terminology or knowledge) to interpret it correctly, has 'filled in' with a set of semantics which may sound impressive to the uninitiated, but are gobbledegook to the real scientist. Let us be kind and say that in the above mentioned case the intentions were well meaning, and perhaps, it was the communicator and not the medium who got the wrong end of the stick. After all, being on the 'other side' does not automatically give the spirit access to information of all kinds. For example, if dear old Aunt Jane passes over she is not guaranteed immediate access to the nature of parallel universes! But think how much more helpful the intended information might have been had the channeller possessed more of the data required to describe accurately events of a cosmic nature taking place in this section of the galaxy at that time. Or had he, she or 'it' simply been playing with a variation of an old episode of Startrek?

Germane to the above is an instance in the past which serves to illustrate my point. I and some friends were present at a gathering at the Marylebone Spiritualist Association (now the Spiritualist Association of Great Britain), when the great medium Horace Hambling was taking the platform *along with three other well-known and highly respected mediums of the time.* Hambling's Guide, Moon

Trail, was renowned for his wisdom, so when the question of reincarnation was put to each of them from a member of the audience, I and my colleagues were eager to hear what they had to say. Three of them admitted to having no memories of having lived before, but Moon Trail, on the other hand, was not only in full agreement on the reincarnation issue but also admitted to having being a Priest in Atlantis, which experience he had cherished lovingly ever since! However, he felt the 'Moon Trail' persona to be more acceptable to people at that time. Needless to say, another member of the audience then put the question to each of the other 'Guides' as to why Moon Trail (or Hambling himself?) enjoyed a much wider knowledge of such matters than they did. They each gave almost exactly the same answer: 'We can only go 'up' so far - Moon Trail can ascend way out of our reach into really high spiritual realms, where, we are told, we will also be able to ascend to when we have learned more.'

Aside from the 'greats' like Hambling and Co., my own list of genuine channellers, (although I doubt whether these gentlemen in question would be too pleased about being included in what they might view as a practise that is anything but scientific) contains such names as Newton, Schweitzer, Einstein, Freud, Jung, Hawking, Penrose, Gribbin, Feynman, Bohm, and other personalities of the last millennium who have added a breadth of vision to our concept of the Universe (well, the one that is comprehensible to the science of today). These people were/are, of course from one or other field of science or medicine, and many of them have indeed been inspired in that they have rendered some valuable service to mankind and the planet as a whole. I have to confess to searching my neural data-banks in vain for suitable names from other disciplines, so any omission could simply be highlighting deficiencies in my own personal areas of knowledge.

Development Circles

Although it has been the practise in spiritualist circles for some years, what I would describe as 'open development circles', where all the sitters are encouraged to 'have a go' can, if the group leader has not been trained in the correct procedures, lead to mental disorientation, or a malfunctioning in that area of the brain which deals with logic. I have been surprised at how few of those taking classes for meditation and development these days know how to ensure that at the end of a session their sitters are properly 'earthed' (their spirits - I prefer the term 'fields' - are correctly re-aligned with their bodies) and their auras are tightly closed!

So what about the art of genuine recognition? During my early days in the metaphysical field I trained several mediums, and one of the things I always taught them was to 'challenge' any external intelligence, and not simply sit down, close their eyes and let it all happen. Any good occultist worth his or her salt can easily detect the presence of a spirit entity, be it a genuine helper, a possible teacher, a mischievous sprite or a malign intelligence of evil (chaotic) intent. And, depending on his/her own ability to distinguish between an evolved soul and a more youthful presence seeking an ego trip, accept or reject the communicator in question. In my twenty years as President of The Atlanteans, this procedure was always carried out with great care and respect. However, after working with a specific external entity for some time, one's brain becomes aware of its presence and duly welcomes it. But, sadly, there are many people in this day and age who choose to call themselves 'occultists', who have not even heard of the Nine Metaphysical Laws, let alone practised them, so there are 'grey' areas on both sides of the mystical polarity!

Ignorance of the need to 'exchange energies', is another example of the kind of occult/spiritual nescience that pervades the metaphysical climate of today. Nothing in the Cosmos is free - all must be paid for in one way or another. Therefore, an effective exchange of energies with supraphysical presences can prove of ultimate benefit to both sides. For example, when 'praying' for assistance, setting up a Rite with the intention of obtaining help with some problem, or requesting a special favour, the correct procedure is to proffer energy from one's own inner resources, thus effecting the balance essential to the efficient functioning of Cosmic Law. (A concept beautifully illustrated in the Biblical Parable of The Talents).

Incidentally, if, from time to time, I do appear to pay due deference to more traditional wisdom-sources, it should not be read that I am 'persuaded' by any of these, but rather that I am trying to employ metaphors which are more likely to be understood by those who favour more orthodox belief systems.

Alien Contacts

Knowledge of the existence of intelligent beings in this and other Universes has been known to occultists and mystics since the time of Mu and Atlantis. In more recent years, the Italian philosopher and cosmologist, Giordano Bruno (1548-1600), was proclaimed a heretic for holding this view. Bruno entered the Dominican Order at the age of 15 but left in 1576 when he was charged with heresy and delivered to the Inquisition. Refusing to recant, he was burned at the stake in 1600. His most important works were a series of dialogues in which he argued for the indivisibility of all matter and all forms, and in which he extended the Copernican thought to state that the Universe is *an Infinite Series of Solar Systems - in space there are numberless Earths circling round other Suns, many of which bear upon them creatures similar or even superior to those upon our human Earth.* Now in my book of rules that is real channelling! And bearing all that in mind, it is little wonder that the Vatican took umbrage!

Taken over several years, one of the main changes which has occurred in the field of trance mediumship/channelling has been the arrival on the scene of 'aliens' from other parts of this galaxy, or our universe at large. Now I am a fervent believer in communication with intelligent beings from other inhabited worlds, but why do so many channellers view such communicators as hominid-type beings? Which begs the question, why do so many people here on Earth still view their God *in their own image and likeness?* Orthodox religion teaches us that God made us in His own image and likeness, but I am inclined to think that it has now become the other way round. Having knowledge of, dealings with, and a former life among beings who are anything but hominid in appearance, does encourage one to consider those hominids who use religion as an excuse to assert their superiority over other life forms, and to view their own kind in terms of the Pharisee rather than the Publican in the Biblical parable - and we all know how that situation was judged! I am told by my own external connections that the 'hominid supremacy myth' is the joke of the galaxy! But then I can offer no proof (well, at present, anyway), as to the truth of this statement. We shall simply have to wait and see, by which time I shall have long departed this Earth!

Although I strive to be as open-minded as possible, my credulity never ceases to be strained by these various 'cosmic councils', which, according to the relevant channellers, are set up along human 'Committee' lines. One is reminded of the words of the late Winston Churchill: 'If Moses had been a Committee, the Israelites would still be in Egypt!' Which seems a suitable point at which to disengage myself from further polemics on this subject.

Relevant to our theme is - well, I think so, anyway - the idea that if a group of people meditate together they can avert major cosmic disasters, or any disaster, come to that. When lecturing on the Gaia theme, for example, and her proposed axis tilt in particular, I have been firmly put in my place with remarks such as 'if we all sit down and meditate we can avert any changes of that nature'. What utter rubbish! If there is a meditation group which possesses such powers, why do they not stop global warming, avert those disasters which deprive millions of their loved ones, homes and livelihoods? Sad to say, the elemental forces always have been, and always will be greater than mankind, and the only way to tame them is not to 'command' them (a mistake often made by magicians), but to merge with them, thus imbibing their knowledge and understanding. All this will eventually happen in the fullness of time; but by then, the hominid species will have achieved its evolutionary goal and be ready to take its leave of Gaia's body, and move to its next stage of cosmic development. Meantime, it is worth heeding the words of Lord Byron:

> Roll, on thou deep and dark blue ocean - roll!
> Ten thousand fleets sweep over thee in vain;
> Man marks the earth with ruin - his control
> Stops with the shore; upon the watery plain
>   The wrecks are all thy deed. Nor doth remain
>   A shadow of man's ravage, save his own,
> When, for a moment, like a drop of rain,
> He sinks into thy depths with bubbling groan,
> Without a grave, unknelled, uncoffined, and UNKNOWN!
>   (Childe Harold)

And so, having done the 'damage', the time has come for some sensible repairs. Because of the highly radioactive natures of their fields (souls), powerful beings from the faster frequencies (other universes) are often obliged to use intermediaries in order to make contact with us lesser mortals. So, no matter how accurate the transmission, if the receiver is faulty, the real facts may become obscured by interference of one kind or another, thus creating yet further impediments in our quest for truth. But surely each person views truth from his/her own personal standpoint or current conviction, which means that changes in our attitude towards it inevitably alter in the light of new perspectives? It can also, at times, prove to be both kind on the one hand and cruel on the other.

Although there may be times when a medium/channeller's facility for the absorption of higher energies is effective, there are other occasions when he/she is, perhaps, not actually receiving anything. However, his/her cerebral data-banks having retained the memory of earlier communications, the tendency is to fall back on these, and, should the 'void' continue, to repeat those same messages over and over again until they degenerate into a series of homespun philosophies which are purely the product of his/her subconscious mind. As long as there are people willing to accept such meanderings the supply will, sadly, continue. In all matters relating to the metaphysical, care should always be taken to avoid falling into those two extremes of New Age psychedelia on the one hand, and rigid adherence to specific fundamentalist dogmas on the other, mental inflexibility of any kind being conducive to cramping the kind of logical thinking required to effect a fair assessment of any material purporting to emanate from extrasensory or supramundane sources.

The Interpretation Factor

There is, however, another side to this 'accuracy' debate which is seldom taken into account, that being the ability of the listeners/ pupils fully to understand what they are being taught. To illustrate my point, I could not do better than heed the Gnostic views regarding who accepts what, and at which level. These wise people saw humankind as being divided into three categories: Hyle, Psyche and Pneuma. Once again I turn to earlier scholarship for my quote from the Theosophical scholar G.R.S.Mead:

> 'Thus it was the custom for them to divide mankind into three classes: (a) the lowest, or "hylics", were those who were so entirely dead to spiritual things that they were as the hyle or unreceptive matter of the world; (b) the intermediate class were

called "psychics", for though believers in things spiritual, they were believers simply, and required miracles and signs to strengthen their faith; whereas the "pneumatics" or spiritual, the highest class, were those capable of knowledge of spiritual matters; those who could receive the Gnosis. It is somewhat the custom in our days, in extreme circles, to claim that all men are "equal". The modern theologian wisely qualifies this claim by the adverb "morally". Thus stated, the idea is by no means a peculiarly Christian view - for the doctrine is common to all the great religions, seeing that it simply asserts the great principle of justice as one of the manifestations of the Deity. The Gnostic view, however, is far clearer, and more in accord with the facts of evolution: it admits the "morally equal", but it further asserts difference of degree, not only in body and soul, but also in spirit, in order to make the morality proportional, and so to carry out the inner meaning of the parable of the talents'.[2]

As I commented in my autobiography 'Oh, had I the courage to write thus!'

Having said my piece, which may appear to the newcomer to my work as being somewhat unkind, it is only fair that I should be asked for some criteria against which to evaluate, and facilitate identification of the level from which a channelling entity is communicating:

a) The breadth of its knowledge/messages/instructions, especially if relating to Cosmic cognition.
b) Its ability to keep one step ahead of modern scientific discoveries, logic demanding that such information, if latterly proven to be accurate, must obviously have emanated from a higher mind/intelligence, which has access to other, more elevated dimensions.
c) Its comprehension of the psychology, stage of spiritual development/understanding, and therefore the needs, of the listeners/enquirers.

In this debate there is one fact that needs to be fairly and squarely faced, that being that even the most honest and spiritually inclined sensitive is going to prove a stumbling-block for those beings who wish to convey any really advanced information if he/she does not possess the appropriate cerebral software. This says much in favour of channellers, and psychics generally, consulting more erudite works in order to familiarise themselves with the terms of reference more appropriate to the message or scenario of the communicator. The logical answer to this problem, (which someone is bound to point out to me), is that an entity or essence with a certain type of information or message to impart, is going to be drawn to someone who they know will be capable of doing justice to their 'teaching' - hence my earlier scientific-cum-medical list. Therefore, what we are really dealing with is the human ego - the medium/channeller, or his/her hominid soul communicators, who aspire to knowledge beyond their limited comprehension, thus causing misinterpretation of cosmic information resulting in confusion all round - our 'photon belt' being a typical example.

Neural software - genetic hardware - these are, of course, purely metaphors of the age, ones which will doubtless be discarded in years to come in favour of some new terminology more relevant to the prevailing zeitgeist. While we are on the subject of the kind of psychic discipline that is encouraging of good mediumship/channelling, it goes without saying that either the use of mind-bending chemical substances/drugs, or over-indulgence in alcohol, can have an adverse effect on the brain, thus limiting the level of contact and impairing considerably the quality of reception. This also applies to those who have chosen the occult path, but more of that in Chapter 11.

I would like to summarise this Chapter by saying that the kind of neural receptivity which is currently labelled 'channelling' is, like every other talent, a gift. We cannot all be literary geniuses, brain surgeons or great leaders. Perhaps, like two of the men in the Parable, we have talents which we can multiply by wise use thereof. Or are we so resentful of the talents of others that, instead of utilising our 'one', we are so aggrieved that not only do we refrain from any effort to double it, but set out to deliberately sabotage the efforts of those who do.

So, bearing in mind that 'like' inevitably attracts 'like', if you, the reader, do possess several gifts, one of which is psychic receptivity, then good luck to you, and may you endear the presence of kind, caring, knowledgeable and responsible entities, who are themselves sufficiently wise to acknowledge both your channelling potential and cerebral limitations. However, if that Path is not for you, but you seek an audience before which to perform, or feel the need for a class you would like to teach, then for goodness sake join the local Amateur Dramatic Society, or take a Teachers Training Course which has been formulated to assist those with learning difficulties. No claps, or gasps of admiration there, I'm afraid, but you can be sure of your accolades in the next dimension.

1   *Where Science and Magic Meet p.142.*, Serena Roney-Dougal, Element Books 1991.
2   *Fragments of a Faith Forgotten*, G.R.S. Mead. 1900.

CHAPTER 3

THE DIVINATORY ARTS AND OTHER POPULAR PRETERNATURAL ACTIVITIES

The Psychic Factor

So often one hears the comment, 'He/she's psychic, you know'. The problem with this blanket term is that it covers a multitude of both virtues and vices, in other words, it can be all things to all people. Taken in the broadest possible sense, and because the aim of this book is to cover all relevant avenues of research which could conceivably offer an insight into the various levels of consciousness involved in the manifestation of what is broadly termed 'psychism', I would describe the psychic faculty, along with all allied metaphysical/preternatural phenomena, as a bi-product of the interplay between time, genetic factors, neural-mechanisms and the 'field' or soul.

Over the ages, mankind has had recourse to innumerable methods of divination, some of which have survived the journey through the millennia and are still in use to this day. Many of today's practising psychics have come to rely on focusing aids such as Tarot Cards, Runes, and the many other systems that have become popularised following the advent of the so-termed 'New Age'. In fact it has become *de rigueur* for well-known psychic practitioners, especially those who have made their mark in one or other branch of the media, to 'invent' their own, special systems. What all of these approaches have in common is that they appear to conform to the Jungian archetypal system, favoured archetypal images varying - albeit unconsciously - according to (a) ethnic background and (b) karmic past.

Observation over many years has inclined me to the view that of the two influential factors mentioned above, (b) does, in fact, exert a stronger effect when it comes to personal preference. For example, those whose soul-fragments have experienced (or are experiencing, if taken in the holographic context), former existences in, say, the North American Continent, tend to be drawn to that ethnic Indian symbology in one form or another; likewise with influences brought over from African, Asian or European sources, which will tend to incline a practitioner towards the archetypal imagery associated with these ethnic locations and the eras in which they predominated. As any psychologist knows, archetypal pictures/designs, etc. work via the unconscious, the symbols presented to the brain being descrambled and their meanings conveyed to the conscious mind in a mode acceptable to present day thinking.

Before we proceed further, I would like to make it clear that it is not my intention in this work to render explanations, detailed descriptions, or *modus operandi* of the different systems. Books on how to read the Tarot, Runes, Animal Cards, or even my own invention, *Cartouche*, are readily available in any shop specialising in metaphysical literature. What I shall try to explain, however, is:

i) How genuine psychism can be seen to function at the four levels enumerated above.
ii) Recognition of those pitfalls which inevitably dog all paranormal pursuits.
iii) Psychic/occult self-defence, or, better still, how to avoid landing oneself in a position where one needs either to extract oneself from a difficult situation, or preferably, avoid such a contingency in the first place.

There is a saying 'to know your enemy is half the battle won', and never does this apply more forcibly than in the metaphysical fields - in all their manifestations.

Clairvoyance

Many clairvoyants choose to dispense with any form of psychological or mystical aid, and work directly through their intuition, unconsciously using their left brains to interpret the impressions received, which they render in a form deemed to be appropriate or acceptable to the querent. The information they impart can therefore vary from precise descriptions, pictures, etc., to psychological-cum-mystical imagery. An in-depth study of these phenomena serves to highlight one positive fact - people with genuine clairvoyant gifts are *able to access time*. In other words, their 'field', 'soul', or whichever name one chooses to describe what is broadly termed 'consciousness', can move both backwards and forwards through time as we know it. However, in spite of what certain 'instruction books' would have us believe, the ability to access time's 'keyholes' is a specific faculty which years of observation have led me to conclude is the peculiar property of a certain gene, and therefore NOT possessed by all and sundry. The level at which this genetic gift is expressed, however, is contingent upon the soul-age (field-band-width), and therefore the 'intention' of the practitioner.

A few months prior to commencing work on this book, I was given a psychic reading by Arthur Molinary from The College of Psychic Studies, a man who, I am sure, must rank among London's best. He was able to describe, among other things, details of my home, my mother and father (my father died when I was only a few days old), the Nanny who raised me, and my Russian grandfather who died in 1908. When it came to the latter, he rendered me knowledge of which I was in no way aware but, when later checked from historically known facts, proved to be 100% accurate. On that score alone (and there were countless others in the reading) there could be no question of his accessing my neural databanks for such information (reading my mind, in common parlance) as there was no such record therein! In the six months following the reading, everything forecast has so far come about. As to the future, well, only time will tell.

So, from a neurological standpoint, how does he function? Which brings us back to Time. It would appear that a certain part of the brain is developed more strongly in some people than in others. In 1996, experiments carried out at Duke University, North Carolina, showed that the striatum, a primitive part of the brain previously thought to control movement only, in addition to being concerned with the human feeling for rhythm, actually keeps track of time to the millisecond! In fact, the brain circuitry that controls our perception of time has been pinpointed, an advance which, according to the scientists involved, will pave the way towards an understanding of why time sometimes seems to fly on the one hand, and drag on the other. Other information obtained from these experiments showed how alcohol and drugs can also change our perception of time, and not always to our advantage! Intelligence, however, as distinct from neural activities generally, is dependent upon our genes, the gene for high intelligence, for example, providing a vital clue in discovering how important DNA is in the development of both intellect and the intuitive faculty.

So, what may we deduce from the above that might have some bearing on the clairvoyant (time accessing) ability? Provided that we carry the genetic factor associated with this unequivocal gift, and the specific area of the brain which allows *the conversion of that information into coherent terms* is well developed, we will exhibit the extraordinary talent of Arthur Molinary, which leads me neatly into the next subject - Remote Viewing.

Remote Viewing

A distinguished scientist, whom I am privileged to count among my friends, has been conducting a series of experiments in Remote Viewing, along the lines of those carried out by a certain military/security organisation in the U.S.A. One such assay involved two people working together, the idea being for one to tune in to the mind of the other to the extent that an accurate description could be rendered of that person's home environment. For one woman in particular this presented no difficulties - unless a positive 'time-slip' is to be viewed as a negative? When tuning in to the habitat of the partner she was allotted for the experiment, she was able to describe his home in detail, including the front door and entry hall, *but as they were when the family in question moved into the house many years earlier.* In other words, what she was actually accessing were the data-banks of the house itself, using the brain of the 'experimental partner' as an entrée.

This, and similar experiments, have tended to confirm the 'field theory' (see Introduction), of which I have long been a proponent, the idea being that every single *thing* has a 'field', which contains the memory of all that has happened to 'it' during its experience in the world of matter. By accessing the data banks of, say, a minute particle, one can therefore ascertain the nature of that particle's 'experience' from, perhaps, a single quark, to its eventual bonding with other particles to create mass.

Germane to this theory is the Eastern practice of Samyama, which allows access to all consciousness throughout time. Eminent scientist Professor Peter Stewart has carried out several experiments which appear to confirm the authenticity of this method, and cites the case of Dr. Barbara McClintock as an example. He tells us that in 1944 Dr.McClintock, a member of the American National Academy of Sciences, 'did more to clean up the cytology of neurospora than all other cytological geneticists had done in all previous time in all forms of mold'. Before the year was out she was elected President of the Genetic Society of America.

The story goes thus: after being offered a post at Stanford University her confidence began to fail, even before she set out to confront the allotted task. She became apprehensive to the point of being 'petrified', that maybe she was taking on more than she could really cope with? Her early work on the project only served to discourage her further; and it was then that she realised something was seriously wrong. In an effort to channel her thoughts into a more constructive mode she took a walk which led her to a group of giant eucalyptus trees. After half an hour on a bench beneath these giant representatives of nature, to use her own term, 'Something happened'. She had somehow learned (from the consciousness of the trees?) to 'integrate' with the object of her research, rather than viewing it purely from the exterior. What she had experienced was Samyama. From that moment on, the more she worked with the chromosomes the 'bigger and bigger they got - and I was really working with them, I wasn't outside, I was right down there with them, I was part of the system ... as you look at these things they become part of you and you forget yourself'. *You forget yourself* - what an important statement, and how very relevant to my ensuing text. Wonderful stuff!

Astral Projection and the Psychic 'Bodies'

The phenomenon referred to as 'astral projection' usually occurs during sleep, although there have been instances of well-attested occurences during surgical procedures, when a part of the consciousness of the anaesthetised person is able to not only observe the actual operation, but also recall later, in detail, the conversations that took place between the surgeons and their attendant nurses. Such phenomena are often dismissed by cynics on the ground that (a) the patient was 'not properly under', or (b) that there is a section of the brain that takes over in such instances and, if the patient's neuro-mechanisms are particularly sharp, can actually effect the recall. In other words, there is nothing paranormal about these events.

On the other hand, examples of experiences undergone during astral projection which have been well documented have latterly been proven correct. So, what are the mechanics involved in these phenomena, are they really 'magical' or purely neural? The idea that an aspect of our consciousness is capable of operating outside of the physical body is as old as the hills. In fact, many ancient schools of metaphysical belief actually subscribe to the idea that one has special 'bodies' designed for negotiating other dimensions. According to the Ancient Egyptians these were as follows:

THE SAHU - or spiritual body - that which is abstract;
THE KHU - or spirit - the magical essence;
THE BA - or soul - probably the etheric body;
THE KA - or double - the astral body;
THE SEKHEM - or 'power';
THE AB - or heart - the seat of the emotions;
THE KHAIBIT - or shadow - the unconscious;
THE REN - or name - the personal sonic;
THE KHAT - or physical body - that which is perishable.

These may be seen to equate with similar classifications rendered by ensuing arcane traditions and systems of transpersonal psychology, (which could refer to either levels of consciousness, or progressively accelerating frequencies), such as Etheric, Astral-Mental, Causal and Spiritual bodies; Atma, Buddha, Manas, Kama, Prana and Rupa; and a similar catalogue of nomenclatures. In my Cartouche system of self-help and divination I ascribed the various Egyptian subtle bodies to nine main divinities, including the epagomenal Neters, as follows: 1. Osiris; 2. Isis; 3. Horus; 4. Bast; 6. Hathor; 7. Nephthys; 8. Ptah; 9.Anubis and 10. Set. I also included Thoth, listing him as card No.5, but allotting the Ibis as his symbol rather than one of the spiritual hieroglyphs. Well, after all, he is Lord of Time, which gives him access to ALL dimensions *simultaneously*!

From my own viewpoint, however, there are no such things as astral (or otherwise) bodies - the image (or cognisance) simply adjusts according to the frequency to which it is exposed. When my consciousness, (soul/field) takes leave of my body in sleep, or when undertaking one of its exploratory 'journeys' through time, it changes automatically, adjusting to each level in much the same way as the holiday-maker leaving Britain in mid-winter for sunnier climes dispenses with his/her seasonal clothing upon arrival.

Psychometry

Accessing the data-banks of objects - that would be my description of this somewhat specialised psychic art. Actually, I have witnessed some first class work in this field over the years. One reader who, when given a plain sealed envelope containing a sliver of wood from the floor of a certain building, was able to describe the selection of the original site by the financier/architect, and the gradual erection of the well-known building itself. In fact, he was quite surprised when the envelope was finally opened to reveal its contents.

During the 1970's, I myself was subjected to a series of 'psychic' tests by a Dr.Carl Sargent, then of Cambridge University. One of these also involved holding a set of 12 plain envelopes, each of which contained a photograph, my task being to describe the *person* in the photograph. Not the sort of test I relish at the best of times! At the end of the session he informed me that he could not accord me 100% accuracy as I had failed in one particular description. When handling the envelope in question, I had sensed the head of a horse, which I described to him. But the envelope was eventually opened to reveal the picture of a young girl, *with her arm around a horse's neck.* Science requiring exactitude at all times, in the eyes of my examiner this constituted a failure. But from my own standpoint it served to confirm my own cosmic background as a Changeling, which would naturally cause me to feel the stronger pull of the horse's soul, which was older than the soul of the human child.

There were countless other tests which always ended up the same way. Among, say, three psychiatrists/psychologists (and on one occasion a brain surgeon!) present, two would be convinced, while the others would ridicule both myself and those who had given credence to my efforts. Often, all of the 'experts' present would be convinced, but when confronted by their colleagues who had not witnessed the experiment, the comments to be overheard usually went thus: 'Okay, so you're hooked, but now we want to have a go, and see this stuff for ourselves. Why should we take your word for it. For all we know you could be on friendly terms with the subject!' After several months of this nonsense I bowed out, never to play guinea-pig again.

But to return to psychometry. Because it deals with the more factual aspects of psychism it is always a good training ground for the aspiring psychic. After all, whatever is being psychometrised (to the pananimist, anyway, and that goes for me) is a real 'presence', and although (as is often the case) an object belonging to a person or persons is used as an *entrée* into the neural databanks of that person, it can render proof of accuracy (or inaccuracy as the case may be).

Astrology

Often referred to as 'the mundane occult sciences', we have Astrology, Palmistry, Numerology, Phrenology, Tarot, Runes and similar systems of divination. But is the psychic faculty actually employed in any of these practices? Astrology, we are told, is an exact science. An astrological chart, for example, if incorrectly erected, can give false information. I commenced my own astrological studies during my teens, and I have to admit that for the first few years my 'calculations' could certainly have been viewed by an 'expert' as highly suspect. These days, of course, I am extremely careful. However, my prognostications seem to work out either way, which suggests the intuitive faculty at work.

Over the years I have studied many charts, especially those of people in the public eye such as politicians, entertainers and royalty. Time and time again I have read the forecasts of the 'experts' in those magazines which are believed to present only *ex cathedra* chart interpretations, unsullied by the 'Mystic Megs' of this world. When subsequent events prove these to be incorrect, one cannot help noticing that little is said in the aftermath, and yet, invariably I have looked at those very charts and foreseen the likelihood of death, fame, or disaster - which has inevitably occurred in the fullness of time. So, while I applaud the genius of many of the great astrologers, I will risk ruffling a few feathers and say that good astrological prognostications are at least fifty percent intuition (psychism, if you prefer), and fifty percent accurate calculations. As for Sun-Sign astrology of the newspaper variety, while it may occasionally hit the nail on the head this is more luck than judgment.

Great astrologers like Newton were able to apply their scientific knowledge to this divinatory art, and, according to some researchers, the famous Elizabethan mage Dr.John Dee calculated, to the moment, when the Spanish Armada would come into view. It was this, and this alone, which was the reason why Sir Francis Drake continued his game of bowls on Plymouth Hoe before taking his ships forth to engage the enemy. But then his monarch, Elizabeth I, was herself a student of the occult arts. But more of that later.

Palmistry

I first read palms when I was in my teens, a practise which, due to my lack of 'psychological finesse', once lost me a close friend. Being somewhat *gauche* in those days, I was befriended by a girl where I worked at the time, who was much more 'with it'. She decided to take pity on me and smarten me up, and we became what I thought at the time to be fairly good friends. One day, however, she caught me reading a book on Palmistry and begged me to read her hand. At the time, she was being courted by a young man and was eagerly anticipating the inevitable engagement ring followed by an early marriage. I recall taking a detailed look at both her palms, but the right hand in particular, and telling her she would have two marriages! (How terribly undiplomatic of me, given the circumstances). She was so furious that she broke off our friendship immediately, married her beau *post-haste* and produced a questionably early baby(!).

It some years before I saw her again. I was in the WAAFS at the time and home for a few days leave. As it happened our local cinema was showing a film which my dear Aunt, with whom I resided, was particularly keen to see. So, I made it my treat. Upon approaching the Box Office, however, I espied my former friend, who seemed highly pleased to see me, greeting me with the words. 'I have been trying to get in touch with you for ages, but I heard that you had left the area. Please may I have a private word with you?' After arranging for another member of the staff to take over for her at the Box Office she joined Auntie and myself in the foyer. In a flood of tears she apologised profusely for having treated me so badly over the palm reading, and hastened to assure me that everything I had told her in my reading had subsequently come true. Her 'husband' had proved to be 'a no good rotter', they had eventually divorced, and she had now met a wonderful man who had recently proposed to her. 'Thanks to you', she told me, 'I now know that my second marriage will be a success'. And so it was.

A salutary lesson for teenage - or older, inexperienced - palmists who would benefit from the study of a little psychology before plunging in at the deep end. Or you could, as in my case, lose a good friend, or even wreck a life!

Numerology

Numerology is, as I have discovered over the years, more of an exact science than an intuitive gamble, although, of course, even interpreting somebody's numbers can be a hit and miss affair. As those mathematicians who are also metaphysicians will hasten to assure us, the Universe is itself a mathematical conundrum. But then they also tell us that mathematics can be applied to all sorts of things in life, including the Bible! Although my own knowledge of the Numerological Art is, I fear, somewhat rudimentary, I have, in some strange way, found it sufficient to guide me through troubled waters on more than one occasion. For example, when in a '9' year, expect things to be taken from you, hitherto hidden problems to jump up and sock you one, and things generally to go wrong or misfire in some unforeseen way. But as mundane numerology tends to work mainly on the one to nine system, at least one can be sure that, having negotiated the end of a '9' cycle and survived, the next year, which will be a '1', will open the door to a new phase in one's life.

Of course there is much more to numerology than this simple example. The Greek sages, and Plato and Pythagoras in particular, paid great attention to its workings. The only comment I can offer is that I, personally, have found it to be a reasonably accurate method of ascertaining facts relative to the material world in particular, although it is also believed to have its 'higher octaves'.

Phrenology

According to Franz Gall, the Founder of Phrenology, different parts of the head correspond to certain talents and behavioural patterns. Although the modern clinical study of neuroscience (about which I shall be writing in a later Chapter) confirms that the head and its contents do affect the human psyche to no mean degree, Gall's feeling for 'bumps' fails to pass the scientific criteria demanded by today's medical knowledge of the subject. Which brings us back full circle to psychism.

My Nanny who raised me, told me of how, at the age of 6, she (and the other seven children in the family into which she had been born) was taken to see a 'wise woman' who read her hand, erected an astrological chart for the time of her birth, and *read her bumps*. The results of both her readings, and those of her siblings, proved accurate to the degree that the paths in life to which each of them were deemed to be the best suited, turned out to be absolutely correct. My Nanny, for example, was told that she would enter the Nursing profession and then switch to being a private Nanny. She assured me on many occasions that she could not have found a more satisfying and fulfilling profession. No doubt, when the Wise Woman was supposedly 'reading her bumps' she was, in fact, tuning in, albeit unconsciously, to those neural mechanisms and their attendant genes, that were suggestive of the Nursing/Nannying mode which brought so much happiness to the life of Nurse Rhoda Adams.

The Tarot and Similar Divinatory Systems

As I stated at the commencement of this Chapter, focussing aids such as the Runes and the many card systems, which are extant among the esoterica of today, are already adequately covered in the instruction booklets which accompany them. Mind you, the innumerable interpretations of the Tarot alone are guaranteed to confuse some beginners, which brings us back to the mind-set, or software of the seeker. So, aside from reinforcing my earlier comments, I see no need for lengthy esoteric or psychological explanations in respect of any of the numerous divinatory 'systems'. In the final analysis, we each find our own level - in both interpretation, and understanding.

A final note: there is, of course, a point at which psychism and occultism merge, which I shall be dealing with later, along with the inevitable question 'How do I know which of the many metaphysical Paths (if any) is the right one for me?'.

CHAPTER 4

THE 'NEW AGE' EPISODE

The Onset Of Chaos

'Follow, follow, follow, the Merry Merry Pipes of Pan' - so goes the song. If only they did follow Pan the world would be a better place and Nature the beneficiary! But let us first tackle the meaning of the term 'New Age'. Was 'it', as many believe, born in 1960? Maybe so, maybe not. But that was certainly the time when I, as a Changeling, became aware that the descent into chaos had undoubtedly commenced, and as Time deftly applied Its foot to the accelerator, the chaotic mode slowly and insidiously commenced to permeate human consciousness.

This is by no means the first time that such a turn of events has occurred, Chaos being the child of Order and Order the child of Chaos. After certain dramatic changes have taken place on this planet, the Gods of Time will release their celestial feet from the chaotic accelerator and apply it to the brakes of Order, for such is the recurring pattern of all existence.

The term 'New Age' has come to mean all things to all people. To some it is viewed as the first steps on the Path to enlightenment; to others, the key to the closet of hedonism. Which path the individual chooses will, of course, depend on his/her soul-age.

To live through a period of accelerating chaos can prove a painful experience for an older soul who has opted for the constructive rather than the destructive approach to change. Chaos does, however, have its pluses in that although it can bring well-established, secure, stable and comfortable modes of existence crashing down, less desirable aspects of life and living are likewise affected. Chaos effects a clean sweep across all borders - nothing or no-one is spared.

When writing in a somewhat derogatory fashion about 'New Age', I was promptly brought to heel by a woman who hastened to point out what a great affect this phenomenon had exerted on 'spirituality'. Well, I suppose it depends where, and for what, you are seeking on the one hand, and the criteria against which you evaluate the stage of the soul's/field's evolution on the other. For example, I doubt very much if elderly pensioners living alone in inner city Council Estates would agree with her (I speak here from first hand experience - I am aged 70 as I write, and I live on a Council Estate!) In days past, the elderly were allowed to live their lives in peace, aided by friendly neighbours, and youngsters who would happily run errands for them, or weed their gardens, for a few pence. Many of today's equivalent of those children/youths who delight in smashing old people's windows and robbing them of what little they have, to support their drug habit - need I go on?

So, where are the so-termed 'spiritual advantages' of this New Age? I, for one, have been hard-pushed to locate them. With the advent of the 60's, people I knew assured me that 'wonderful, advanced souls would be born into the world - souls who were destined to bring enlightenment to all, and thus raise the standard of living world-wide'. Several of those who believed implicitly in this premise duly gave birth - to spiritually orientated Bringers of Light? Hardly. One here and there, no doubt, but the overall picture fails to fulfil the expectation.

Having sat back over the years and watched the progress of some of these so-termed, 'great souls', what I have witnessed is drug-dealing, hedonism, selfishness, money-mania and a complete abandonment of self-discipline on the one hand, and the 'follow, follow, follow' syndrome on the other. And the worst is still to come!

The Guru Cult

Earlier in this narrative, I commented on the need felt by some people to 'follow' something - be it a cult, or simply some figure perceived by them to be 'spiritual'. Likewise there are those who have elected to forfeit their mental freedom somewhere along the path of spiritual domination, or ethical preference. Sometimes such compulsions can be so overpowering that they becomes obsessional, adherents to specific cults, for example, tending to shelve all personal responsibility on to a cult Leader, or Guru, as the case may be. Evidence of the chaotic side of this phenomenon may be observed in the many cult calamities which have resulted in mass murders. 'Ah', you will say, 'But people followed Jesus, and it didn't seem to do them any harm - and likewise there are many Gurus who have brought enlightenment and peace of mind to people worldwide, and young souls in particular'. Well, as to the former, those who were tortured to death during the many Inquisitions might not agree with you, and with the latter, one supposes there are a few here and there who have benefited in some way from their encounters.

All right, so some young souls feel the need to avoid personal/ethical responsibility by passing this over to a religion or cult of one kind or another. However, the problem facing us all lies in the fact that the spiritual evolution of the soul/field of Gaia herself, (Danuih to me!) has outstripped, or outpaced that of the majority of humans at present living on Her surface. Since in this instance it is She who holds the reins of Time, and in order to effect Her own progress she will be obliged (with the aid of other external forces) to effect a massive culling, her 'permit' to stay being issued only to those whose stage of cosmic awareness is compatible with her own. In other words, she will not allow humanity to hold her back. Harsh words, but true, I fear. After all, she has done it many times before, as may be evidenced in the extinction of the saurians, among other, long-gone species.

A New Age there will indeed be, but not in the drug-sodden, airy-fairy, indisciplined, violent, destructive mode of today. It is a rather gentle, caring society that waits in the wings of Time, the members of which have finally come to realise that ALL forms of life are equal, and that the hominid supremacy myth is, simply, a myth! However, as Jung tells us, there is a lesson to be learned from all myths and the sooner humanity realises this, the better it will be for all the life-forms that Danuih 'chooses to embrace' in the future. By that time, the present, so-termed 'New Age' will have become 'old hat'.

But to return to the guru-cult, as long as people are prepared to assign responsibility for their personal, spiritual progression to another, there will be gurus. Relieve them of that need (as Danuih will surely do in the future), and the gurus will be no more. Perhaps self-discipline has become a dirty word in certain quarters, but on the other hand excessive discipline, hours of chanting, and avoiding the 'real' world, are just as much a manifestation of Chaos as the opposite. In the final analysis, the 'middle path' is usually the wisest in the long run.

Self-Discovery and the Meditative Practices

Many people with whom I have discussed the subject of meditation have assured me that they are 'seeking the self within'. In fact, self-seeking seems to have become the 'in' thing these days. Personally, I am on Dr.McClintock's side here (see Chapter 3), experience having taught me that the best way to discover one's 'self' is by comparison on the one hand, and blending with other fields (souls), either incarnate or discarnate, throughout time, on the other. I am reminded of a series of psychology lectures I attended in my youth when the elderly lecturer, a doctor of psychology, brought the attention of his students to a certain set of characteristics which he irreverently referred to as 'The Ooslem Bird Syndrome'. This he viewed as an aberration which he associated with those people who were so obsessed with self-discovery that they were inevitably destined for the same fate as the fabled 'Ooslem Bird' (which it would not befit me to enlarge upon in a book of this nature!)

Self-seeking can become a spiritual trap in that it emphasises the 'self' rather than the role played by the 'self' in the Universal scheme of things. Those who have contributed to the well being of all life in this world have usually tended to place more emphasis on what they can do for others rather than how they can help themselves. Surely there is a lesson to be learned in this? I recently questioned a very dear friend of mine, (who is the nearest person I have ever met to the sainted Mother Teresa), on this very subject. Her answer? 'I never think of myself, I just 'do', and in doing I find my real vocation'.

Viewed from another perspective, however, it has ever been the way in Eastern mysticism to search within, although this could only be seen to apply to those who have failed to establish their spiritual identities by way of more external approaches to the *Gestalt*? For my own part, if I need to know how a tree is feeling, whether one of my beloved cats is suffering, or whether friends I have not heard from for some time are well or ill, it behoves me to tune in to them, to become one with their feelings, fears, etc., and in so doing, forget myself. In fact I can recall one day when I was far from well, but, being concerned for the health of a friend, I pushed my own discomfort to one side and sent her healing. This resulted not only in her effecting a speedy recovery, but my own malaise suddenly taking a turn for the better!

The same logic can also be applied to the many who sit round for long periods meditating on the Earth and sending her 'healing'. As she said to me during my conversations with her (see *The Gaia Dialogues*), she would rather that those well-intentioned people effected some practical help such as cleaning up the environment, caring for the other creatures that are her children, and acknowledging the equality of all to whom or to which she gives succour and life on her body, our world.

The Butterfly Syndrome

Here is another of my former Lecturer's collection, which as the years go past, has popped up and hit me under the chin on more than one occasion. Why so, you may ask? Well, I am constantly meeting people who, knowing my interest in matters esoteric, hasten to enlighten me as to the many organisations they have belonged to over the years, and the inordinate number of classes/ workshops/ seminars they have attended during this period. Such people are seldom, if ever, without some literature relevant to their current quest, which they hasten to produce from a handbag, shopping bag or briefcase. However, when questioned as to the philosophy, teaching, or general information gained from these multitudinous informatory encounters their memory conveniently alludes them. What they do usually recall, however, is that 'The Speaker was fabulous - so persuasive, so interesting, SO inspiring', similar paeans of praise being duly bestowed upon most of the other 'Teachers' encountered in preceding years. I usually end up by asking 'But what have *you yourself* learned from all this - has it helped you to understand life's *raison d'etre*, the nature of the Universe, death, the past?' Had I a pound for each of those who felt that their continual search had finally brought them the peace of spiritual/cosmic understanding, I might just be able to afford the odd tin of cat food for my beloved five! When mentioning my stance on this subject to a recent acquaintance it was pointed out to me that the only way some people learn is by 'doing the rounds', because if they fail to get the message during this life, it may have been imbibed at another level and will thus serve them well in their next. Put into that context I suppose it does make some sense, although I still have my doubts.

Walk-Ins

Following the publication of certain reading material on this subject, 'Walk-Ins' seem to be popping up all over the place. It strikes me as strange that these phenomena didn't appear to exist prior to the publication of the literature in question. But then it is rather like the UFO phenomenon: in my youth, aliens were beautiful Venusians as described by George Adamski, with long, flowing fair hair, golden skin, and blue or golden eyes! But since the publication of a certain book, which featured an alien of somewhat different visage, (reproductions of which were subsequently to be seen on every rubbish-bin and lamp-post around), numerous people claiming to have been 'abducted' were immediately able to describe the chappie on the posters!

Years ago, of course, great mystics like Thomas the Rhymer (Thomas of Ercaldoune), effected their disappearing acts by paying a visit (or being invited as the case may be) to the kingdom of Mab, Queen of the Fairies, wherein they dwelt for two whole years (or whatever!) in 'Outer Time' (the timeless state), which often amounted to one night only in 'Inner Time', (the time we see on our clocks).

But I digress. Our subject matter in this instance is 'Walk-Ins'. It would seem that some people who are in the process of treading the mystical Path find that after, say, a few years, they wake up one morning feeling quite a different person, as if some *one*, or some *thing* has taken them over. Having looked carefully into several such stories, and then allowed an aspect of my own consciousness (field) to take a look, I see no alien, but rather another aspect, or fragment, of that person's own soul/field, usually one which is slightly more advanced than the earlier resident. But aliens? No way. My own Teacher used to liken an advanced soul to a reservoir of water, only a few drops (soul fragments) of which would enter a human body at any one time. Were we to take too much on board without due preparation, the brain would be incapable of coping and mental illness, or even death, could result. Hence the need for slow Initiation into the higher cosmic wave-bands, which subject I shall be dealing with in the Chapters on occultism/magic.

Perhaps it might help if I explained the 'Fragment Theory', a belief which is upheld by several metaphysicians of learning and note. Having examined the linear incarnation premise I found that it simply did not add up, although for many years I was unable to offer a viable alternative. More study, experience and observation was needed, both from a logical viewpoint, and also allowing for the numerous NDE's and similar out-of-the-body experiences collected by researchers of integrity and repute such as Eysenck and Sargent. It was Dr.Lyall Watson who finally provided me with the clue I needed in his 'shattered hologram theory', in which he conceives of the whole Essence (field or soul), or the combined aspects of the quantum self, in terms of a complete hologram which becomes shattered and its fragments *simultaneously* scattered across all periods of time and across the limitless dimensions of all universes. Since every piece contains the same, albeit indistinctive in some cases, image of the whole, a fraction (wave/particle) of the essential self is retained in every life, and it is that connection with the basic essence which has given rise to the concept of a 'higher', or transpersonal Self. We are therefore experiencing some lives as youthful fragments, and others in intermediate or mature modes.

Over vast eons of Inner Time these fragments slowly come together (return from chaos to order) to complete the whole, this chaos/order process being repeated into infinity. However, it is possible for a piece of that hologram existing in, say, the year 3000 A.D., to connect with, or overshadow its fellow in the present, thus creating an Einstein on the one hand, or a possible 'Walk-In' on the other. These, or similar connections, are simply aspects of the one soul (hologram) rather than saintly beings or aliens in today's general understanding of these terms. However - and here is one for the prophetic books - having myself looked into the future of life on this Earth in millennia to come, I have seen a race of beautiful people with golden-brown skins, blue or golden slanted eyes, and long, flowing fair hair - a combination, perhaps, of all the races extant in our world today *who fitted, in every detail, Adamski's 'Venusians'*. So were Adamski's originals ACTUALLY EARTH

HOMINIDS FROM THE FUTURE, TIME-TRAVELLING (FOR A HISTORY LESSON, MAYBE), TO THE PAST? The crosscurrents of Time being what they are, it bears consideration.

These theories are, of course, at variance with the popular belief espoused by many schools of mystical belief which conceive of a series of incarnations through linear or Inner Time, which would accord with the concept of Time's forward arrow. In other words, they are viewing Time in its compartmentalising aspect only. But how many of these doctrines are conversant with the true nature of Time, and with *that point in the speed of Time at which all Time exists simultaneously?*

Animals, being for the most part wiser than humans (wasn't it the late Johnny Morris who said: 'Humans are clever; animals are *intelligent*'), and therefore well aware of the existence of their other fragments, negotiate Time's innumerable frequencies naturally and without aforethought. My cats, for instance. When obliged to take their leave of me due to accident, old age, or illness, these dear creatures having bonded with me so closely, soon find a body in which, or through which to return. For example, Pearl, my beautiful chinchilla girl, who, anticipating her fate (she was savaged by a dog and died of her wounds), had *already selected a new body,* which she made sure would be ready for collection within a week of her passing. Now was that a 'Walk-In', or was it that one of her fragments was already ensconced in the little white fluffy body of my new kitten, Thoth (Tottie). Well, I simply had to name him after the Egyptian God of Time, didn't I?

What I do know is that Pearl walked into the body of Tottie, but, in effecting this takeover, did she require the resident soul to leave (or did it leave voluntarily by previous agreement as the 'walk-in' doctrine would have us believe?) Neither! You see, both the furry person that was Pearl before, and the little kitten that is Tottie now, are both aspects or fragments of that whole feline soul-field. All Pearl did was to reinforce the Tottie soul with another fragment from the central field-bank that constitutes that whole of that field of consciousness. The same applies to people although, sadly, in some cases it is not always an aspect of the 'higher self' that invades the present scenario. As any psychiatrist will confirm, like inevitably attracting like, sudden personality changes are not always precipitated by or from 'spiritual' sources!

So, if you feel yourself to be a 'Walk-In', and the benefits of the change are positive, don't worry too much about what has happened to the previous 'tenant', or holographic fragment of your whole field which, deeming the time to be right for a spiritual transition, has simply become absorbed into the existing 'you'!

As previously mentioned, I am a Changeling, which means that my soul/field is that of a Time Deva, and not of the hominid species. Our kind only take on human bodies for specific reasons. Anyone interested in this subject will find a full explanation in my autobiography *The Changeling,* which was published by The College of Psychic Studies in May of 1999. Incidentally, I did not evict a human soul in order to take over this body. I took it over at conception, as is the custom among my kind. Any psychic worth his or her salt can, from the moment of conception, easily tell whether a woman is pregnant by the presence of a second (or more) soul/field. I ran a Healing Group in Central London for over 20 years, and there are friends of mine around today who can vouch for what I say. One, in fact, when told she was pregnant in her forties, could not believe it, and it was not until her doctor confirmed the fact that she was able to accept it!

As for those supposedly undesirable aliens, well, a little knowledge of psychic self defence could soon put paid to them - if your psychiatrist hasn't done so already!

CHAPTER 5

THE HEALING ARTS

Healing - Vocation, Gift or 'Acquisition'?

Are healers born or 'made'? This is a question I am often asked, but is there an answer that will satisfy all those who aspire to embrace the healing arts? So many well-intentioned people, all eager to do good in some form or another, feel that they would like to become healers or Counsellors, the latter, which I shall be dealing with later in this Chapter, being particularly favoured in certain sections of society. A vocational calling of this kind may well result in those who are fired by the enthusiasm of both doing good and enjoying the process to boot, being drawn to the study of one or more of the popular 'alternative therapies' which tend to require less formal training than that demanded by established medical standards. 'Healing', however, is something of a 'blanket' term, in that it covers a host of therapies ranging from conventional medical treatments to the 'alternatives', some of which are excellent, others more suspect. While it can be argued that not every student who emerges from medical school with a degree is automatically a good healer, the same can be said of the amateur who naturally assumes that taking the relevant Course, (which is often pricey, to say the least), and meeting the standards set by the organisation in question, automatically makes him/her a 'healer'.

Healing is a 'gift', and one which, sadly to say, cannot be bought. As I have mentioned previously, I ran a Healing Group in Central London for years, along with Gillian Kings (now deceased), an Anglo-Burmese girl who was the epitome of a natural healer. When I left the Group to pursue other areas of my metaphysical studies, those who took over effected a complete revamp of the whole metaphysical system which I had taught. This naturally affected the Healing side; what was viewed as an appropriate 'Course' being drawn up for participation by paid students. Although a few 'extras' were added, counselling being one of these, the *modus operandi* appeared to be the same as that employed by Gillian and myself during the previous years. The main difference, however, was that when I ran that organisation there was no charge for healing, either for the recipient or the student healer.

The occasion subsequently arose when one of my 'senior' healers, who had not participated in the new 'Course', was told that she could not heal with the group until she had taken the mandatory Course (and paid the appropriate fee, no doubt), in spite of the fact that she was on a par with Gillian when it came to producing the required healing results. Taken in this context, I, too, would probably have been excluded from that healing scenario, although I was the originator of many of the techniques used, which I remembered from my life in Atlantis.

I still do the occasional healing case to this day, for both humans and animals, but my calling has now alerted me to new fields of endeavour, so whether or not I am required to produce a well-paid-for 'certificate', is no longer of relevance.

Healing is, like all other 'talents', a specific 'gift' which one either has or has not. All the courses in the world will not remedy this. Many animals possess it, but sadly, not all those humans who fancy themselves as being gifted are thus blessed. At this point, I should like to quote from my book *Cosmic Connections*, in which I was privileged to enjoy a dialogue with the Devic Essence of the Planetoid Chiron, known in mythology as 'The Wounded Healer'. The conversation went thus (my question in the first instance):

Murry: Does everyone possess healing skills? I hear certain New Age people suggesting that these skills lie dormant in all hominids, and can therefore be surfaced by undertaking a few courses or seminars.

Chiron: I fear that those who attend such courses are sadly misguided by their egos, while those who arrange them are either genuinely ignorant of Cosmic Law or more concerned with their Bank Accounts than the effect such beliefs may have on gullible young fields (souls). May I put it to you (and them) this way: is everyone a great artist, singer, mathematician, surgeon, etc.? Of course not. Each member of the human race is blessed with certain gifts which the field has deemed essential for negotiation in its present existence. These gifts, or 'frequency-negotiabilities' as I prefer to call them, differ considerably with the individual. As to the healing facility - as you would say, the proof of the pudding inevitably lies in the eating. The ability to self-heal is something that eventually comes with the expansion of field-band-width, or spiritual maturity if you prefer, the truly wise person knowing exactly when to make use of this faculty and when the time has come to let go and pass on. As I see it, one of the problems with healing in your world today is that it has become too compartmentalised. The surgeon is separated from the general practitioner, the medical profession as a whole from complementary medicine and alternative therapies, and so on. Of course there are those people who are able to effect the healing process because the nature of their field is such that it can channel certain cosmic frequencies, via the brain, which can assist in the balancing of chaos/order factors in human (and other) bodies. The genuinely gifted healer does this instinctively, without the need for quick-sale seminars and the like, while there are many among the medical profession itself who do it naturally, every day, and not necessarily via the prescriptions they are expected to hand out. So, although study and practical experience can obviously improve performance, healers, my dear friend, are, like good doctors, good teachers, and good psychics/occultists, born, not 'bought' or 'made'.

Murry: Thank you Chiron. That one is, I fear, going to put the proverbial cats among the pigeons, but I have no intention of watering it down to please certain elements in 'society'.

Chiron: Good. And now a final word of advice, prompted by your reference to pigeons. There are, among the animal world, many skilled healers. Cats, in particular, can help the mentally afflicted, so can fish, while among dogs and horses there are those who carry out their corrective skills in more practical ways. Think about it ...'[1]

Since Chiron has been one of my teachers, I could not hope to better his words. However, when it comes to a specific, and brutally fatal disease, there is something I would like to bring to the notice of not only those who claim specific paranormal healing powers, but also the medical profession itself.

The Cancer Enigma

One of the most disturbing diseases to afflict mankind (and many other life forms, for that matter), is the dreaded big 'C'. Many years ago when I worked as a Healer, I was quick to recognise that cancer was, in fact, an invading 'field' or alien entity. In other words, it was a 'soul' from a very low life-form which was totally alien to this planet, but had somehow become lost, and was therefore looking for suitable hosts upon which to feed. But then it can be argued that the human body is host to all manner of 'alien' entities, some of which belong there, and others not, the relationship between these 'lodgers' and their host needing to be delicately balanced if illness is to be avoided. But cancer is, it would seem, something of a different 'kettle-of-fish'.

When I first made my discovery I had little or no evidence to add credence to the idea, until one evening, when my husband of the time and I were sitting quietly listening to the radio, there was a sudden and agitated knock on the door of our flat. We opened it to find the nurse, who lived in the flat upstairs, in a state of considerable distress, and needing to unburden the trauma of an experience she had just undergone. She had been working with an oncologist (cancer specialist) at the time, and a patient, who had just died, had signed his body over for medical research. Anxious to discover more about the invading growth which had, in this case, occupied the liver, the surgeon hastily removed the organ in question and placed it on a nearby slab. Fascinated by the process, our nurse peered closely at the organ and its 'occupant' and, to her horror, *it was pulsating - a living being - its life-span outliving that of its host by minutes!* When the nurse expressed fear and horror at what she saw her employer coldly remarked, 'I've seen bigger ones that that, some of which have survived up to five minutes or more after the death of the patient!' This fact was also confirmed for me recently by a friend who had several years of experience as a theatre nurse.

It was then that I realised I was right. The cancer entity is an alien field which invades the human body, which naturally invites the question, 'Why some more than others?' I have heard it said that people who are subconsciously seeking an 'exit door' emit a neural signal which attracts killer 'fields'. But there are altogether too many 'buts' in this premise, although when it comes to the matter of life and death, perhaps the veneer of civilisation beneath which we so trepidly hide, is actually concealing the light of truth - or are there still pockets of illumination on this sad planet which have somehow managed to evade the chaotic tentacles of time by coping with the death syndrome in a painless and more civilised way? I refer to a TV documentary some years ago which featured a tribe of people living somewhere on the Indian sub-continent, the members of which, having divined when their time is up, gather their loved ones around them and bid them farewell, with a promise to return (if necessary) at some future date. They then pass peacefully away - no agony, no doctors, no painful drugs or surgery.

As a member of the Scientific and Medical Network, I recently received a copy of their magazine *Net Work* which contained one particular article that commanded my immediate attention, *Cancer and Morphogenetic Fields*, by Eli Erich Lasch, of Berlin, in which he affirms that cancer is, in fact, an alien field or soul.

Fields, of course, as I have explained in so many of my books, come in all shapes and sizes, the latter being designated by their 'age' or band-width. In metaphysics one frequently hears such terms as 'old soul', 'young soul' and so forth, the fields of the older souls inevitably displaying much wider band-widths than their juniors. In Atlantis, the Priesthood were always elected on the grounds of their soul age - what an improvement on today's criteria, when leaders appear to be chosen for their TV images, bank balances, media contacts, or associations with one or other section of society. The terms 'younger' and 'older', however, should not be viewed within the framework of time as we know it, but taken in a far wider context.

The human body, as with all life-forms, has ever been under attack from invading alien fields of one kind or another. Our history books tell of plagues, massive flu epidemics, rampant tuberculosis, and so forth, each in turn, being tackled by the medical science of the day (or dealt with by people's own immune systems). A slow honing of the genes, perhaps, or a series of salutary lessons on how not to treat the physical body?

To return to our original subject - cancer. The article to which I mentioned is both lengthy and highly technical, so it has been difficult for me to choose extracts from it which would be easy for the layman to comprehend. Herr Lasch asserts that cancer cells are not sick cells, but young and primitive ones, the more primitive of these being responsible for the most malignant tumours. In fact, they appear to exhibit a kind of 'immortality', which may be evidenced in the fact that there are tissue cultures in existence which go back to the 1940's. Herr Lasch is a spiritual healer, specialising in morphic fields, and one comment in particular caught my eye:

> When many years ago I was confronted for the first time with a case of breast cancer I was astonished to realise that there exists a defect in the field overlying the tumour. Not only that, but a cool "breeze" seemed to be coming out of that defect. While any other disease and especially pain and inflammation feels "hot", cancer gives a feeling of "cold". This is something I have found in over ninety per cent of cancer cases, and which most of my students, as well as some journalists, have also felt.

As a former exorcist I can vouch for the fact that the presence of an alien entity (field), especially one of more primitive (lesser evolved) origin, inevitably gives off a 'chill' in much the same way that a haunted house can send shivers up and down one's spine. When dealing with healing cases involving cancerous entities, Gillian and I always used the 'caller/coverer system', in which she would effect a mental protection around me while I removed the alien spirit from its host. I would then signal to her to switch her cover to the 'patient', thus ensuring that the invader could not return thereto. I was then free to guide the intruder to a cosmic environment more congenial to its kind, thus leaving the patient's natural resources free to effect a physical adjustment.

'But', you may ask, 'over the years you must surely have come to recognise the nature and origin of these invaders, and therefore where to return them to when exorcising them?' Yes, I was able to identify those cancerous entities with which I dealt as type of 'field' which originally occupied a form of succulent plant life on a planet which was no longer able to support any form of vegetation. Time and time again I found myself associating them with our Moon. Unless returned to a more suitable cosmic environment such entities will, as Herr Lasch has indicated, appear to reproduce themselves forever, this pattern representing their desperate need to complete a specific cycle via the agency of matter. In other words, what we are basically dealing with is a persistent colony of chaotic lost souls. And as to where I sent those alien fields, well, from the human standpoint, the size of this Universe is almost incomprehensible, and there are innumerable other Universes parallel to ours, and existing in frequencies beyond our limited knowledge.

Another of Herr Lasch's assertions was that one cannot destroy a field. After all, the human soul is nothing more or less than a field and, once in existence, fields inevitably expand via the process of connecting with other fields and gaining information therefrom. But what one can do is to manipulate a troublesome field by moving it on, or returning it to its correct sphere which, in the case of a cancerous field, would mean steering it towards an environment in which it could express itself in a more congenial, physical way. As the Paschats always said: 'Chaos, or evil as you prefer to call it, is simply energy which has become out of place, and there is usually some reason for it being attracted to a certain person, situation, or planet'. But then, my perspective being essentially devic, I tend to view this whole cancer problem as either one of the hominid species 'great initiations', or a possible learning curve perhaps? However, I shall be covering the subject of Exorcism in a subsequent Chapter, when my personal experiences as an exorcist might serve to throw some light on a few of these 'field' enigmas.

A psychologist, who is also a dear friend of mine, once told me, 'There is a definite psychological type which would seem to be more prone to cancer, and likewise with contrasting diseases and other psychological categories.' And now yet another factor relevant to the cancer enigma has come to light. Professor Sir David Lane, working in the field of DNA, has discovered a single gene now known best by its number, p53. The following quote is from the relevant article, which appeared in the *Mail on Sunday Review* (January 23rd, 2000):

> P53 is an extraordinary gene. It is the body's final gatekeeper: if it is present and healthy, cells do not become malignant even if severely provoked by the modern world's vast armoury of carcinogenics. We all have p53 and if yours is healthy, you are highly unlikely to develop cancer.

Journalist Peter Hillmore, who interviewed Professor Lane and wrote the article, commented on p53: 'Is it the body's guardian angel?' However, until such times as Professor Lane's conclusions have been thoroughly tested we are still confronted by the Big 'C' bogey, so are there any other measures which could be employed to cope with the elimination of alien fields? The employment of sonics is one suggestion that has been rumoured, although today's comprehension of this science would appear to be in its infancy when compared with the knowledge of the long-dead past. But on what grounds do I make this statement? Back in the late 1970's I was privileged to be taken to lunch by an elderly gentleman who was a former Nobel Prize Winner. A confirmed metaphysicist, he told me that he had fond memories of being a sonics priest in Atlantis, which prompted me to ask the question, 'Can you also recall the *modus operandi* for its use?' 'Of course I can,' he replied. 'But I would not dream of imparting such knowledge to the world at this stage in its development. Soon I shall be leaving this body, but in times to come, when the human race (or what is left of it) has become sufficiently chastened, I shall return and make such knowledge available'.

It has also been intimated recently that certain electrical frequencies are conducive to somatic malfunctions, the presence of pylons, for example, with mobile phones being the latest 'bogey' to raise its head. I seem to recall Rudolph Steiner having something to say about this. But what if there is also a curative side to electro-magnetism, which could, perhaps, depend on which end of the electro-magnetic spectrum one is dealing with? Just a hint! As a Changeling I am extremely uncomfortable with the lower frequencies of the electromagnetic scale, whereas X-Rays, and radioactivity of any sort, energises me - it is as though I 'feed' from it. Two hours on an X-Ray table and I come out feeling 200%! But this is because I have a field which is alien to that of the normal hominid, being more elemental (Devic) than human. It is this 'devic ray' that I usually applied to cancer entities (fields) when removing them from a patient. One cannot help wondering whether some of the radio-therapy treatment given to cancer patients, while it is designed to destroy the cancer cells, doesn't actually *feed the alien field*? But, lacking the appropriate medical and scientific qualifications, who am I to say; although it makes one think.

Having glimpsed the future of this planet, however, I can offer the following words of hope: cancer, along with a whole range of viral and other illnesses, will be eradicated following radical upheavals and changes destined to take place in this, our new millennium, which will, in turn, effect radical metamorphoses in the DNA of all who survive these turbulences.

The Counselling Craze

These days the counselling 'packet' seems to come in all shapes and sizes, from school children being rushed to counsellors when a member of their class dies, to those long-drawn-out sessions which provide a convenient leaning post for those disinclined to accept responsibility for their own lives. In my youth, when confronted by a frightening situation, one talked it out with one's friends, had a good moan, and soon forgot about it. Furthermore, I am not referring simply to the inevitable teenage problems, but also to the witnessing of bombs dropping around one, homes set alight by falling incendiaries, and the mangled bodies of loved ones strewn around. One expects such horrors on the battlefield, but in one's home environment, well ...

Some years ago I was discussing healing with someone with whom I had worked in my original Group, only to be told that their 'healing package' now included counselling. 'But why?', I asked. 'Because', I was told, 'it is essential to the holistic and curative procedure.' While I can go along with the 'comfort' side of counselling, I felt the need to question its efficacy as a curer of diseases, and found myself asking my companion whom she believed to be the greatest Healer of all times. 'Why, Jesus, of course!', she replied with alacrity, which prompted my riposte, 'But I do not seem to recall His use of counselling in the performance of His healing miracles - was there not the incident of the woman who touched the hem of His garment and was immediately cured, with a caution about sins being forgiven (karma absolved?) And another where a man begged for help for his dying daughter in a distant town only to be told immediately that from that moment she would live - and she did? Such healings were instantaneous and required no counselling sessions to seal their efficacy. Well, for any Christian the obvious answer is that that He was someone rather special, and not our present day run-of-the-mill therapist. But whichever stance one elects to employ in this debate I still maintain that Counselling, cosy as it may seem, is purely a palliative, and therefore not an ingredient essential to the healing process. I, for one, would like to meet a Counsellor who has actually cured a cancer patient by talking things out with them!

I do concede, however, that Counselling does have a psychological role to play in providing an outlet for the expression of pent-up emotion on the one hand, and the chance for people to get something off their chest, on the other; and in these specific areas in particular, there are many people who have a desperate need of its services. However, there are still quite a few among us 'oldies' who prefer to effect a little 'pulling oneself together', rather than baring one's soul to someone who has taken a few weeks course on how to offer a shoulder to cry on!.

I think this is an appropriate point to take leave of our subject-matter; but before my readers hasten to create a picture of your author which borders on the flippant, let me hasten to assure them that I have effected a life-long study of healing, and illness generally. Anyone who has received healing at my hands, or studied in one of my healing classes, will, I am sure, be only too happy to endorse my sincerity when it comes to suffering of any kind, and the multitudinous approaches to the healing arts with which mankind has employed over the centuries to combat its disturbing and painful effects.

Therapies - Their Use and Abuse

It would take several tomes to cover the innumerable methods of healing employed throughout the world in this day and age, but for those interested, my *Psychology of Healing* (available through the Public Library System) renders broad definitions of such practices as conventional medicine, the psychologies, manipulative medicine, the humanistic and transpersonal psychologies, the physiological therapies, Behaviourism, paranormal therapies, oriental therapies, and many, many more.

I am, however, reminded of one instance when I was lecturing in the USA. A lady approached me who had recently undergone a process known as 'Rebirthing', which involves the patient being held under water for a period believed to correspond to the prenatal environment, and then 're-birthed', the idea being that any trauma associated with one's entry into this world can be thus cleared. From her paean of praise for this 'act' I assumed she had recently undergone said experience so, out of interest, and assuming it to be a 'first', I asked her what effect it had produced. She replied,'You mean *this* time?' Which prompted my response, 'Why, have you had recourse to this procedure on more than one occasion?' 'Why, sure', she answered. 'Fifteen times so far. It's sure fun, and you get a different 'high' each time!' No comment.

Rebirthing can, however, be conducive to abreaction, and in once instance which was brought to my attention the side-effects were so violent that the rebirthing team were unable to cope and had to call in the assistance of a doctor (fortunately, there happened to be one nearby!) who subdued the hysterical woman with the traditional 'hand slap'.

Certain therapies appear to suit some people more than others; kinesiology, for example, does nothing for me but works wonders for a friend of mine, while reflexology sends me way off into the hinterlands of time, wherein I usually enjoy a welcome respite from the woes of this planet. So, in the final analysis, it would appear to be a question of what achieves the best results for whom.

A recent article in YOU magazine (one of the 'accessories' of *The Mail on Sunday*), on the subject of Therapies caught my eye. It featured an interview with Psychiatrist Professor Anthony Clare, MB, B.Ch., BAO, M.Phil., in which the question was put to him; 'Do you feel everyone could be helped by a spell of therapy?' He replied: 'Therapy is for those who are ill, or in need of assistance and help. I'm a bit suspicious of therapy junkies who go from one practice to another because they're searching for something therapy can't give them - the sense that they're loved. It becomes a substitute relationship, something other people find in their marriages or with their children or friends, or it becomes a kind of religion. Really you should get what you can out of it and move on.' My sentiments, precisely.

A final comment which will, no doubt, go down like a lead balloon with some of my readers. I referred earlier to expensive Healing Courses, many of which are far beyond the resources of those who might well be blessed with healing powers. In fact, as I was writing this Chapter, a dear friend rang me and, in the process of the conversation, told me about a wonderful healer in her area whose successes are well attested to, but who has never attended a Healing Course of any kind. In orthodox medicine, an appropriate degree is obviously called for, doctors being frequently confronted by life-death situations, any mistake, no matter how small, being answerable to the Law of the Land. On the other hand the gift of what is broadly referred to as 'psychic' or 'spiritual' healing cannot be bought, and calling oneself a 'Grand Master', or some similar ego-flattering appellation, is no guarantee of one's prowess in the Healing Arts. However, one cannot help asking, as I and my friends do time and time again, why are such titles so sought after? The answer must surely lie in one small word - ego.

1   See *Cosmic Connections* page 146-147

CHAPTER 6

RELIGION, PSYCHISM AND THE SPIRITUALITY TRAP

The Definition of 'Belief'

In this day and age, when moral standards have declined and the dark aura of chaos is slowly and insidiously spreading its sinuous cloak across the moral framework of humanity, it behoves us to seek for inlets of Light wherever, and whenever possible. Over the past few centuries, the great religions of the world have held full sway, minor belief systems being quashed either by persecution and torture, or humiliation and derision. To this day there are fundamentalists who would kill for their beliefs, while the situation in Northern Ireland is a prime example of two branches of the one faith ready to shed the blood of those who fail to toe a similar line.

In one of my many dictionaries Religion is described thus:

1. The expression of man's belief and reverence for a superhuman power or powers regarded as creating or governing the Universe:
2. Any personal or institutionalised system of beliefs or practices embodying this belief or reverence: *The Hindu Religion.*
3. The spiritual or emotional attitude of one who recognises the existence of a superhuman power or powers.
4. Any objective pursued with zeal or conscientious devotion: *A collector might make a religion of his hobby.*
5. The monastic way of life.
6. *Archaic.* Sacred rites or practices. [Middle English *religion*, from Old French *religion*, from Latin *religio* (stem *religion*), bond between man and the gods, perhaps from *religare*, to bind back: [*re-*, back + *ligare*, to bind, fasten.] In other words, the word itself would appear to have many connotations aside from those generally accepted in today's world.

As I see it, religion is not, or never was, created by God or The Gods but by the collective needs of the people at any given stage in the hominid evolutionary cycle. As a result, the Rites and practices associated with each school of belief can be dated to the ethos predominating at its inception, and although it has become fashionable in this day and age to update both the traditional written word, and the original ceremonial, the old neural software still holds sway among many people. There is therefore no 'one truth' as such, each dogma being appropriate to the age in which it first manifests. As humanity progresses and changes, so, also, does the interpretation of The Truth.

When one usually employs the term 'religion' in conversation, it is naturally assumed to relate to one of the great religions of today such as Christianity, Judaism, Islam, Hinduism, Sikhism, Buddhism in its many forms, and so forth. However, taking the meaning of the word as postulated above, one should also include the various branches of Paganism and Wicca and perhaps one or two of the more rational belief-systems which have made their appearance during the last two centuries such as Theosophy, Anthroposophy, as well as the Jungian and the later transpersonal schools of psychology. So what we are really dealing with is a sort of blanket term which can be employed to embrace anything vaguely associated with belief in a force external or superior to the purely physical.

People often ask me whether I believe in this or that. My answer is that I do not believe in *belief*, I either know or I do not know. Belief, for me anyway, implies acceptance of a condition, situation or ethical system which defies my own sense of logic. Drawing on my own field experience as a Changeling, the real forces that govern this, and all other Universes *ad infinitum*, are archetypal, their constants being dependent upon the conditions prevalent in each section of those domains over which they effect their observances. And even these great Devas, Archangels, Neters, or whichever term one finds appropriate, are themselves still learning and evolving.

But, you may ask, is there a God at the head of this celestial hierarchy? It has recently been stated that contemporary developments in astro-physics serve to prove the existence of a Supreme Creator, but not necessarily a single entity; a concentrated, creative energy, perhaps, which works in concert with genetics, neurology, the human psyche, and all fields of consciousness for that matter, be they animal, vegetable, or mineral - a wise father/mother does not favour one child more than another. Then there are the myriad other universes to be taken into consideration - worlds beyond the dreams or imagination of the majority of humankind; are all these battalions of infinity also under the same command?

It is all very well sitting in a professorial chair pontificating on this and that, but if you have not actually experienced the subject matter of your Theses, against which criteria can you validate them? As a devic field who has actually been around more than one universe I can help out a little here, but I must make it clear that I do not possess *all* the answers. What I can do, hopefully, is to render a different *perspective*.

From my personal standpoint, however, I am happy to continue my slow, forward-winding Path, enjoying each revelation of 'cosmic order' as it presents itself, or enduring the suffering inevitably inflicted by 'chaos' with stoicism and resignation (Hobson's Choice, as they say!) During my cosmic travels I have encountered many 'gods', some created by the imagination of men, others genuine Devas or Neters, intent upon their allotted roles in the dance of Creation.

The human soul (field) differs considerably from the devic field, its frequencies being complementary to, but not of, its fellow travellers in the world of matter. The devas create the conditions conducive to human, animal, plant, and all other forms of physical experience, without which the celestial evolutionary blueprint would fail to reach fulfilment. And within the realisation of this genesis the creators, too, are learning their 'trade'.

The Psychic Factor

So, where does psychism enter into this picture? Let us first consider this from the standpoint of orthodox religion. Whether one's preternatural utterances are accepted by the czars of the major religions would seem to depend very much on whether one does one's 'thing' under their auspices, in which case one might well find oneself a candidate for Beautification or even Canonisation providing, of course, one says the right things as appropriate to the relevant belief system. But produce identical phenomena, and belong to an opposing religious camp or, for one's sins, no religion at all, and the witch-hunters move speedily and stealthily into action.

While on the subject of religious phenomena, one is reminded of the following statement from the Acts of the Apostles (2: 2-4) -

> And suddenly there came a sound from heaven, as of a rushing wind, and it filled all the house where they were sitting. And there appeared unto them cloven tongues as of fire, and it sat upon each of them. And they were all filled with the Holy Ghost and began to speak in other tongues, as the spirit gave them utterance.

St. Paul made it clear in his Epistle to the Corinthians that he fervently believed in the need for the Holy Spirit to repeat its Pentecostal visit by descending on Christian congregations from time to time, and while the glossolalia might come as an unexpected bonus, this spirit possession (the Holy Spirit, naturally!), was inevitably the deciding factor in Christian divination and healing.

As an outsider, I cannot help viewing with a degree of suspicion the fact that the spirit possession which takes place in a Church is automatically born on the right side of the heavenly blanket, while anyone claiming spirit guidance outside of that sacerdotal canopy is either mentally ill, possessed of the devil, or fails to qualify as a son or daughter of the Celestial Father (sorry, Mother also now - see later in this Chapter!).

In the psychological context (or somatic, for that matter, bearing in mind the nature of the brain as a computer!), there is little difference, if any, between the alleluias of the Christian evangelical fundamentalists and the ecstatic dances of the Dervishes, while the utterances of the entranced shaman, or Delphic Pythoness, could be equated with glossolalia. The Christian mystic's vision of Christ and the yogi's samadhi are both fashioned in the same ecstatic mould. The autonomic nervous system does not distinguish between Christian or pagan, Muslim or yogi, shaman or saint when registering the somatic reactions of ecstasy. But then, are not ecstasy and frenzy but a hair's breadth apart?

RELIGION, PSYCHISM AND THE SPIRITUALITY TRAP   71

It can be argued that those who either indulge in the gift of tongues, or effect any contact with energies exterior to the physical norm (the channelling phenomena or the saint's glimpse of a Christian heaven), are grasping at collective unconscious race-memories of earlier cultures. The psychologist would, no doubt, prefer Jung's diagnosis of cryptemnesia as the more logical explanation, as his research revealed that among the gibberish which normally passes as glossolalia there was the odd word from another language which was probably registered subconsciously at some earlier point in life - or are our genes speaking again? Xenolalia, or paranormal speaking in real languages, is apparently still unproven, as not a single case has been recorded since the advent of tape-recorders or computers.

Stigmata is another of these religion-orientated psychic-type phenomena which bears out only too well the effect of doctrinal software on the brain, in that many of its claimants manifest bleeding in the centre of their palms when, in fact, the nails of crucifixion were, I am given to understand, always passed through the wrists! Why don't they get their statues right?

The conclusion to be drawn from the above is, sadly, that there are still schools of thought which view any form of psychism undertaken outside the portals of orthodoxy as issuing from evil sources of one kind or another. So, although there is no burning at the stake these days, the flaming arrows of verbal abuse can be just as damning (and painful), and where certain branches of the media are concerned, the humiliating tones of some intellectual journalist/broadcaster can be as agonising to the mind as the searing flames of the pyre or the stifling, mud-ridden waters of the local pond!

I speak from first-hand experience here, having suffered verbal martyrdom on more than one occasion. As a result, it is no longer my policy to make myself available for radio or TV programmes. Even those better read and educated than myself, who dare to step onto certain 'forbidden territories' find themselves lampooned, with relevant sections of their interviews conveniently omitted, and so forth.

I recently watched a BBC programme which was supposed to examine the facts regarding the possibility of there actually being an advanced civilisation prior to the advent of Dynastic Egypt.

Graham Hancock, whose work/research I greatly admire, was ridiculed to the point that his years of patient research were made to look like some school-boy's 'Favourite Yarns'. Being the gentleman that he is, he was polite enough to accept the put-down gracefully. I shudder to think what I would have done in the circumstances, but whatever my riposte it would, of course, have been conveniently extracted from the televised version shown to the public. In fact, this actually happened to me during a broadcast, the subject matter of which was the work of Hancock, myself, and others researching in the field of advanced prehistoric civilisations. Although Graham was booked to be on the panel in question, a last minute accident prevented his attendance and the producer was obliged to make use of a 'phone connection with another author of note. The broadcast was, of course, pre-recorded.

When it came to the subject of Atlantis I duly performed my piece, quoting the *Timaeus and Critias* with which (or so it seemed), the interviewer was unfamiliar. He cut me off in mid-stream, and that was to be the end of my meagre contribution. When the session was finally played over the air my offering had been completely axed. At the time there were workmen installing a new central heating system in my bungalow and, knowing I was 'on the radio', they made a point of listening to the relevant programme. Realising what had happened, on my return they were wholly sympathetic, their opinion of the BBC, and that interviewer in particular, being totally unprintable!

However, all of the orthodox religions would appear to be well represented in the visual media, although one is, occasionally, allowed a glimpse of some ardent pagans doing their stuff at Stonehenge or similar ancient sites at the appropriate times of the year. Sadly, such fleeting visions are usually accompanied by a 'send-up', which, if not expressed verbally, is usually made more than clear by the odd cynical grimace, or effected gesture of amusement.

During my years of 'incarceration' in two ghastly, 'Dickensian' Catholic orphanages, I had it drummed into me that the one uniting factor in Roman Catholicism was its adherence to the old Latin in all its offices. Because of this, we were told, a Catholic could attend Mass in any country in the world and join in the service. Much as I questioned ninety-nine per cent of the other stuff I was taught, that one premise sounded both logical and practical. Fortunately, I had long since abandoned the portals of Catholicism by the time this practice was conveniently scrapped (another instance of political correctness, no doubt), and it was a Jesuit, of all people, who commented sadly to me how this change had, in fact, broken the ritual power of the Mass. Only the old Latin Tridentine retained its power at the Consecration, he told me and, with my own knowledge of the effect of ritual on the human psyche, I agreed with him completely.

But that is not all. I quote from a comment, which appeared in the *Daily Mail* in the summer of 1999, the headline of which read: 'The Pope slams the pearly gates'. It read thus:

> For those expecting to be welcomed by a St.Peter, paradise has just been postponed. Because Heaven isn't quite the place we may have been led to believe, says the Pope. We must not imagine fluffy clouds and angels playing harps in the sky, according to the Pontiff. Instead, we should think of heaven as 'a state of being' after death.
>
> John Paul II told pilgrims outside the Vatican: 'The Heaven in which we will find ourselves is neither an abstraction or a physical place among the clouds.' Instead, he added, it is a 'living and personal relationship with the Holy Trinity and a blessed community of those who remained faithful to Jesus Christ in their lifetime, and are now at one with His glory'.
>
> It was bad news, of course, for the traditional images of art and literature - from Michaelangelo to William Blake - which held out the prospect of a shining celestial city.
>
> However, the 79-year-old Pope's remarks earlier this year may have given a hint of the revised Heavenly image. Then he declared that Christians should stop picturing God as 'an old man with a white beard' and instead see him as a Supreme Being with masculine and feminine aspects.
>
> The traditional image of Hell is cooling down a little as well. The magazine of the Jesuits say it is not all fire and brimstone.
>
> Instead, it is a state of being in which those who had rejected God and 'consciously chosen not to do good' would be excluded from God's presence forever.

Well, well, what can I say - times certainly change!

During my conversation with Gaia (Danuih, to me - see *The Gaia Dialogues*), on behalf of a friend I put the question to her as to why she never 'appeared' to anyone in the way claimed by certain 'saints', to render prophecies or words of spiritual encouragement. She assured me that she had assumed a human form in order to make contact with people on several occasions, but had given up in the end because these appearances 'usually ended up as statues in Catholic Churches'.

Of course, Christianity today has many branches which range from the strictly orthodox (no women priests) to the 'happy-clappies', who appear to express their religious ardour in something akin to a pop concert. I have spoken to some people who attend such events, not out of religious ardour, but simply to 'let their hair down' and, as one young man put it 'have a good time'. Which of these approaches is the most 'spiritual'? The Parable of the Good Samaritan springs to mind or 'by their deeds shall ye know them'. Of course young souls, like young children, will ever indulge in noisy play, but the time inevitably comes when we all have to grow up and that means, among other considerations, questioning the true nature of the Deity (Deities), the most respectful (or joyful?) way to approach It (Them), and Its (Their) responses to our unending litany of petitions for this and that.

The Church of England does, however, appear to be broadening its horizons as far as psychism is concerned, as may be evidenced in the following comment, which appeared in the *Daily Mail* on 18th December 1999: 'Each Diocese in England retains an advisor on paranormal activities' because the Church 'takes these beliefs very seriously'. Is it too early to applaud?

But as to whether psychism manifests through the agency of orthodoxy, or whether it is simply Madame Arcati doing her stuff, whichever level the operating sensitive attains to, or is inspired from, will be governed by the frequency he/she is able to negotiate on the one hand, and the intention behind the 'service' on the other. I have often heard it said of this or that medium 'Oh, she's good on the practical stuff, but if you want something a bit more uplifting, you should have a sitting with Mr. S. He's more on the spiritual side'. Horses for Courses, as the saying goes, all levels proving beneficial if the 'aim to help' is genuine.

Wiccan, Pagan and Celtic Approaches

Since Roman Catholicism has been the only religion with which I have had any contact, I do not feel entitled to comment on any other world faith. However, I would like to put in a word for those who have chosen more 'nature-orientated' paths of worship, Pagans and Wiccans, for example, while there are others who still elect to follow the old Celtic ways. Thanks (or no thanks) to Christianity, Paganism, and what is often (and erroneously) referred to as 'Witchcraft', seem to have attracted bad reputations over the years and it is only since the Witchcraft Act was repealed in 1951 that Witches, Pagans, and other Goddess worshippers, have been able to practise their belief-systems openly and without fear of prosecution. (And with nary a forked tail or cloven hoof in sight!). Sadly, to this day, many dictionaries, erroneously define The Craft as 'Black Magic' and 'Devil Worship', so there are still those unenlightened (or uneducated?) people who conceive of witches as being 'in league with the devil', which is ridiculous, since genuine Wiccans do not accept the existence of such an entity.

According to Wiccan beliefs -

i) The female principle is deified and designated equal to or greater than the male.
ii) Body and Soul are seen as one and the same; one cannot exist without the other.
iii) Nature is sacred and not to be abused or 'conquered'.
iv) The individual has intrinsic value and is not to be subordinated to the 'revealed' will of the deity.
v) Time is circular and repetitive; existence is cyclic; the figures of the Triple Goddess symbolize constant repetitions of growth and decay.
vi) There is no original sin, and no hard and fast separation of 'good' and 'evil'...
vii) Sexuality, spontaneity, humour and play activities may be incorporated into ritual, where the experience of pleasure is regarded as a positive force in life, rather than the temptation of sin. [1]

Likewise the old Celtic ways, which have undergone a revival in recent years, also acknowledge the Triple Goddess in Her many forms and Her Divine Partner, while also acceding to mankind's equality with Nature and ALL living things. (A comprehensive account of the history and religion of the ancient Celts can be found in my book *The Ancient Wisdom of the Celts* (see Bibliography). In fact, over the past few decades there has been a resurgence of Paganism generally, especially among the 'greens', and I suppose that, as a pananimist, I must see myself as counted among their number. However, all these schools of belief are deserving of more time and space than this work allows.

As the word 'Wicca' is believed to have derived from the old Anglo-Saxon word meaning 'wise', some schools of thought designate Wiccan practices as having originated in the 'old ways', when there was a 'Wise woman' (Witch), or man (Wizard), in every village, who dispensed herbs and healing balms for people and animals alike. However, the Wiccan aspect of paganism underwent a form of 'modernisation' in recent years, the two major factions which came to prominence being the Gardnerian and the Alexandrian schools of The Craft. Since there is adequate information in print concerning both of these 'camps', I would refer my readers to a list of appropriate literature (which will appear with the Bibliography) kindly compiled for me by a dear friend who is also a competent and knowledgeable occultist, which more than covers the subject. There are, of course, many other groups, the Druids for example, each with their own versions of British Paganism and associated ancient belief-systems from many other countries.

However, to return to the 'bogeymen'. In times long past Chaos assumed many guises, notably Set in ancient Egypt and Ahriman in Zoroastrianism. The ruler of Dante's Inferno, however, would seem to be essentially a Christian creation. Most of the ancient civilisations, in fact, accepted the existence of the chaotic element in creation, to which they paid due deference, probably more out of fear than love. But then, as any scientist will confirm, Chaos does have an essential role to play in the Universal scheme of things.

There are, however, some practitioners of what are commonly referred to as 'the Dark Arts' (occultists who prefer to court the forces of Chaos), while references to 'the devil and his works' still crop up from time to time. I can recall my late Nanny - who was an old pagan if ever there was one - commenting to a visitor who happened to mention 'Old Nick', 'Who's he when he's out?' in typical cockney fashion! Bless her!

The Spirituality Trap

It would be wrong of me to leave my reader with the impression that the only paths to spirituality are via religious orthodoxy on the one hand, or paganism in its many manifestations on the other. I have even come across exclusive groups which practise the religions of ancient Egypt, Celtica, Sumeria and Ancient Greece, among others, each paying due deference to the god-forms extant in these belief-systems. However, when questioned regarding their choice, one discovers that what they are really seeking is *their own spirituality*. In recent years there have been books and articles written on 'women's spirituality', 'men's spirituality', 'gay spirituality', and so forth, but what does the term 'spirituality' *actually mean?* All things to all people, or so it would seem.

I recently conducted a small survey of my own, enquiring of everyone I knew, and members of the general public with whom I have been able to engage in conversation on the subject, what was their understanding of the term. The answers, which ranged from the orthodox to the way-out, seemed to indicate some innate need for communion with a sublime Deity who dispenses justice, love and understanding, choices ranging from Gaia (the Spirit of the Earth) to those inevitable Gurus who claim divine descent. Sadly, as I have emphasised in an earlier Chapter, that spiritual search for the 'self' so often backfires, and therein lies the undoing of many. This 'divine Being' whose good offices they seek, is not, as even the Pope now admits, in some pearly-gated Olympus, but everywhere, all around, in *every living thing*. May I render my reader two examples which were given to me by a genuine Eastern guru some years back.

A certain wise and educated man of the East became preoccupied with the idea of finding God, an obsession which so overpowered his soul that he felt obliged to dedicate his whole life to this spiritual quest. So, on one particular night, having made adequate provision for his wife and child, he rose quietly from his bed and set out on his chosen mission. As year after year passed, the object of his quest seemed to become more and more elusive and, slowly and laboriously the ravages of time alerted him to the inevitable, and he realised his time of departure from this Earth was upon him. Having seated himself beneath the sheltering arms of a fine tree he spent his final hours reminiscing on where he had gone wrong in his search. And in his anguish he cried out to God: 'God, I have made it my life's work to seek thee, and in so doing I have given up much, and suffered much during the pursuit of this quest. Tell me, Oh Divine One, where have I gone wrong?' And the voice of God then spoke to him thus: 'My son, you left me the day you left your wife and child'.

Here is a similar tale from the same source: another greatly respected guru also set himself the task of seeking God whom, he thought, must surely reside somewhere very beautiful. One day, while resting from his travels, he espied a magnificent stone. So beautiful was this rock that the guru thought to himself 'God must surely dwell beneath it'. So he lifted the stone and, becoming so entranced by its beauty, he carried it away as his prize find, completely forgetting to check whether God was, in fact, in residence there.

These two salutary tales say so much to me: I wonder if they will do the same for some, at least, of my readers? Their message is, like my own, that the spirit of the Divine, in no matter which guise we elect to clothe it, is within *everything*. And why not, since He, She or It Created ALL!

So often have I come across this kind of false spirituality. People who never miss Sunday services but, like the Priest in the parable, will gladly look the other way should they pass an injured animal, or fail to check up on a lonely neighbour who has been dead for three days because she was 'not one of us'. One cannot acquire spirituality by listening to endless sermons, attending every available seminar on the subject, reading numerous books or listening to endless tapes. Real spirituality is expressed through action - how you *really* are and what you *DO* in your everyday life. How you treat your fellow human beings, animals, the Earth Herself, the plant kingdoms. 'By their deeds shall ye know them'. Over the years I have been subjected to hours of spiritual claptrap from people who conveniently forget one's spell in hospital, or the fact that when

RELIGION, PSYCHISM AND THE SPIRITUALITY TRAP

their neighbour is sick he/she is unable to shop for him/herself. The essential prerequisites of true spirituality are surely kindness, caring, generosity of spirit, a love of *all* creatures - no matter who or what you believe created them in the first place - sincere reserve, and gratitude to this Universe which offers us the opportunity and freedom of choice to experience, and thus to evolve. And, finally, let us find the humility to vanquish that last great human ego-trip - the hominid superiority myth.

1   *The Woman's Encyclopaedia of Myths and Secrets*, Barbara G. Walker, p.1090.

CHAPTER 7

REINCARNATION, GENETIC MEMORY, DREAMS AND PARALLEL UNIVERSES

The Karma Hypothesis

Although the concept of reincarnation, with its accompanying karmic overtones, has become very popular in this day and age, it has also given rise to some rather debatable ethics, as in the case of a certain sports personality who made the grave (politically incorrect) error of referring to a particular person's physical disability as resulting from past misdeeds. On the other hand, it is quite acceptable for such afflictions to be classified by members of the medical profession as 'genetic' and, taking into consideration that our genes may well predispose us to certain 'discomforts' in the present, how do we know that we were not among those erring ancestors of the past?

In order to make some sense of this duality we need to focus on the roles played by both determinants, which begs the question - at which point do our genes give way to karma, or is it *vice versa?* The answer, of course, lies in the fact that the texture of both our genetic heritage, and our karma, are so closely woven that one automatically becomes the vehicle for the expression of the other. So, has our karma actually attracted us to a body that carries genes, the physical manifestation of which are likely to proclaim either our former virtues or indiscretions? I realise that I am treading on very dangerous ground here, but someone has to say it and, as the saying goes, I might as well be hung for a sheep as for a lamb.

Perhaps the best way to tackle this very delicate subject is to effect a definition of terms as understood in different cultures, commencing with reincarnation. Closely associated with the reincarnation premise is the concept of Karma, which has its seeds in Hinduism and Buddhism, wherein it is defined as the principle of retributive justice determining a person's state of life and his or her incarnations as the effect of past deeds. The concept of punitive Karma, which is based on the 'As ye sow so shall ye reap' principle, can also be read as a popular metaphysical variation of the 'sins of the fathers' theme, the idea being that we will be required to atone for those misdeeds we have perpetrated in previous lives (assuming an acceptance of the linear reincarnation theory which, as has previously been emphasised in this work, your author does not!)

The karmic expiatory process is generally believed to be undertaken in any of several ways:

1. Transmutation of karma through service to a principle in whichever guise one may see fit to acknowledge it (i.e. a favoured ideal, religious calling, sociological humanitarianism, art, and so forth);
2. Realisation of the suffering one has previously imposed on others by taking on a similar condition oneself;
3. Effecting family connections with the mentally or physically disabled which require great personal sacrifice;
4. Entering life with congenital/genetic defects which throw one onto the mercy of others for care and protection; or,
5. Working in a field in which one subconsciously feels one has wronged others.

In my book *The Psychology of Healing*, I gave several examples of the above which I had personally encountered during my years in Healing and Social Work, with the comment that I did not think for one moment that our psyches (consciousness or fields) rationalise their choice of suffering in the sense that this is fed to the soma with subconscious instructions as to the location of the 'eject' button. What seems more likely is the PK (psychokinesis) theory favoured by parapsychologists and some philosophers - that when we experience feelings of despair or disillusionment with what life has to offer us, we exude a certain PK frequency, the quality of which attracts energies of a similar nature. If one's mind has designated these to be negative, destructive or terminal, then what we may draw unto ourselves will also be of a negative, destructive or terminal nature. Certain recent clinical studies have suggested that cancer, for example, is frequently an alternative to despair - and yet, time and time again the media highlights the sad tales of people whom life has favoured with every blessing - a happy family, plenty of money, fame, a zest for life and so forth - being struck down at a comparatively early age for what would appear to be no logical reason. Can all such cases qualify for karmic classification? So many unanswered questions perhaps, but insert the genetic factor, and a somewhat different picture emerges.

Enter the Genes

In the ancient Chinese cult of Ancestor Worship, it was firmly believed that the physical ancestors (genetic predecessors) conspired to make us what we are, but this belief was carried further in that the spirits of the Ancestors were also there for us, to help us through those difficulties which we might have incurred from our deeds in other existences. I recall one occasion when I was attending a stand at the Festival of Mind, Body and Spirit in London, when a benign elderly Chinaman requested my advice on a specific subject, which I was able to give him. In return he told me that although I would be facing hard times in the future, I had very powerful ancestors who would see me through all the trials and stresses that awaited me.

However, taken in the context of the Holographic Theory, which I have covered in Chapter 4, we could just as well be paying for our sins *in the future* as in the past! But now we are entering the realms of timelessness which I, as a Time Deva, might find easy to comprehend, but which those who have yet to reach an understanding of the true nature of time might find mind-boggling, to say the least.

Whether we like it or not, genetic memory does influence our lives, inclining us to be drawn to cultures other than the one into which we have been born this time round. For example, I have encountered several people who feel a strong affinity with the North American Indian ethos, and likewise others who cannot get enough of Ancient Egypt, Rome, Celtica, or wherever. This naturally raises the questions, (a) did all of these actually experience former lives in those cultures, or (b) can their genetic ancestry be traced thereto?

In my books *Atlantis, Myth or Reality* and *The Ancient Wisdom of the Celts*, I carried out an in-depth study of blood groups, which I believed, might serve to throw some light on (a) the existence of the former, and (b) the origins of the latter. Recent studies in genetics have broadened these horizons even further, and, no doubt, by the time the Genome Project has been completed, all of us will have access to information regarding the true nature of our far-distant ancestry.

Is there a genetic blueprint for each of our lives and, bearing in mind the true nature of Time which, as I have explained earlier, *simultaneously* encompasses the past, present and the future, is that blueprint contingent upon our deeds in any of these times or their equivalent dimensions, and where does free will fit into the equation? Taking these questions in *gestalt* the answer to the initial enquiry must, of course, be 'yes'. For a civilisation so reliant upon 'inner time' (the time we see on our clocks) this must appear mind-boggling, coming to terms with one life and one time frequency being about as much as many can handle. Introduce the concept of evolution *ad infinitum* and younger souls will beat a hasty retreat to the cosiness of one life as viewed through the eyes of orthodox religion.

Times inevitably change and, with the advent of certain forthcoming events which are destined to take place in this solar system, human consciousness will be elevated, via neural and genetic reprogramming, to a new and more inter-time notion of existence. As for free will, any doctrines which suggest that Earth is the only planet of choice are questionable, the concept appearing to be incongruous if viewed in the light of the limitations that are inevitably imposed upon its assertion and the obvious presence of the chaotic element which is prerequisite to ethical selection. The expression of free will in the generally accepted meaning of the word is, of course, incidental to such factors as the overall evolution of the home planet, environmental conditions, genetics, cerebral hardware, and other somatic considerations, in addition to the soul-age/field band-width of the individual at each given stage along the path towards full conscious cosmic awareness. In spite of these apparent anomalies, the whole evolutionary process in all its aspects is inevitably contingent upon the expression of some degree of preference, *all* life-forms effecting that option in discriminating between order/chaos, kindness/cruelty, etc. in accordance with the limitations imposed by the boundaries of each level through which they pass on their evolutionary journey. I hesitate to use the terms 'good' and 'evil', since moral attitudes inevitably change as one progresses; perhaps positive/constructive, and negative/destructive might be more appropriate.

However, there are subtle variations on the 'choice' theme. For example, those souls/fields or essences that are still bound to their respective 'collective' (group soul) do not necessarily choose their bodies as is popularly supposed. Rather, they are subconsciously drawn to situations which either allow them to gain the experiences necessary for field expansion, or simply to return to where they were before, and where they therefore feel comfortable. Only individuated souls/essences can effect this specific choice, and these can be easily identified by their attitude towards other species, both on Earth and in other areas of our Universe.

As things stand at the moment, the evolutionary impetus is concerned with the albeit subconscious/unconscious effort to continually update the cerebral software, while also effecting a fuller, and more relatively appropriate use of the hardware (genetic material) available at any one period in time, in as many dimensions as the band-width of the field (life force, essence, soul) allows. In simple terms, most people will accept what they see as reasonable and logical and ignore that which does not conform to their current concept of the 'norm', until such times as first-hand experience, or currently ratified scientific evidence, suggests that things might be otherwise. Even so, bearing in mind that the flat-earth theory still appeals to some members of modern society, in the final analysis we all tend to believe what suits us at any given time.

Genetic Memory

As a firm believer in 'many lives throughout time', I have, of course, had numerous experiences which have served to back this up. Although I have never visited Russia, I had known for some years that my biological grandfather was the Grand Duke Alexei Alexandrovich, fourth son of Csar Alexander II. Even prior to receiving this information I was always deeply moved by anything Russian, my first physical experience of bilocation, in fact, involving a Russian scenario. One evening, when seated comfortably at home in my flat in Cheltenham with my three cats gathered around me, I suddenly found myself at a theatre in St.Petersburg (I just knew that was where it was) during the latter part of the 19th century. The orchestra was tuning up for the performance of a ballet, and I was looking at two people who were occupying one of the 'privileged' boxes. The man was obviously an aristocrat of some status as was his companion, a stunningly beautiful fair-haired lady. There also appeared to be two servants (footmen?) hovering in the background. So real was this scenario that I could actually feel the icy draught that was coming from beneath the thick curtains at the rear of the box, while a combination of the aromas of scent, and unusual food, assailed my nostrils. The two people present were, from my viewpoint, as concrete as anyone in my present-day life, yet it was not some former existence that I had strayed into but my genetic past. In other words, I had unconsciously accessed one aspect of my genetic databanks, and although my present body was still seated comfortably with my cats, each scenario was as solid and earthy as the other, and each sensory appreciation positive in both cases.

It is only in recent times that a photograph of my grandfather has come into my possession and I have been able to recognise him as the Russian gentleman at the ballet. One up for the genes! Now what I do know, and am absolutely sure about, is that *I have never had a physical incarnation in Russia, or anywhere else in Europe for that matter, my one former life on this planet having been in what I affectionately choose to call 'The Old Country - Atlantis'.* (see my Autobiography, *The Changeling*) I have fairly comprehensive recall of at least some of my former existences as a deva, commencing with my identification with a neutrino (minute particle without mass) which was ultimately destined to widen its field by a continual process of accretion both non-local (the quantum worlds) and subsequently in the worlds of matter, when I first ventured into a solid body as a Paschat or Eyani.

In the light of the above, I would therefore caution would-be past-life seekers to consider their genes as an added factor in any memories their consciousness may cause to surface from time to time. After all, how much do we *really* know about our ancestors and, to add a little lightness to the subject, there is an old saying in England that the English are all descended from Edward the Confessor whom, we are given to understand, was more than liberal with his seed! Well, let's face it, the population in those days was somewhat sparser than it is today!

Dreams and Parallel Universes

People who are believers in the concept of parallel universes often ask me how one can access these interdimensional spheres. My answer is, of course, that they are probably doing it all the time - during sleep. How many of my readers have dreamed of living at a certain location which bears no resemblance to any place previously seen or known? And what about dreams of the future which actually come about - are these 'fashioned' in another aeon of time?

In a recent dream I found myself in what I took to be a school classroom. On the wall before me was stretched a map of the world similar to those we had at my old educational establishment. There, sure enough, were the continents as we see them on our maps today, *but the colour distribution was entirely different.* I knew then that I had stumbled into a world which was a paradigm of Earth - some parallel universe which was functioning at a slightly different periodicity from the one we know, thus rendering it invisible to the human eye - *in which evolution had followed an entirely different pattern.* There had been no World Wars I or II, and the colours on the map indicated that the various countries were governed by three main powers. At this point I feel it necessary to refrain from saying which and how, as I would, for sure, be casting a lethal gauntlet before the champions of political correctness. However, given the choice, I know which world I would prefer to live in, and it would not be the one inhabited by the body whose hands are typing this script!

There have been many other instances which have convinced me that an aspect of my field is also negotiating other time-levels of this planet's existence, and other planets/universes no doubt, perhaps as a respite from the stresses of life as it is on Earth today. I can hear the psychologists effecting their 'obviously compensatory' chant - '*a modus operandi* for escape from the trials, tribulations and frustrations of everyday life'. A good way of 'earthing' a problem, no doubt, but the single-dimensional nature of certain areas of modern psychology can also serve to effect limitations which do not, in fact, exist!

While I was writing this very Chapter, I received a letter from a young man who has an Honours Degree in Science, and is at present working as an Occupational Therapist in Scotland. As it concerned an exorcism *carried out in a dream*, I felt it worthy of inclusion at this point:

> I was in Nelson, New Zealand, on the second month of my travels when I had a peculiarly vivid dream. I found myself in a crowd of courtiers, mostly women, I think, among whom a queenly lady was circulating. I noticed that one of the women, though hominid in body, had very canine facial features that I knew to be those of a dog called Staffy (a Staffordshire Bull-Terrier Bitch) who lived with a close friend of mine. Around her feet was running a small black pig-like creature, snapping blindly and viciously at all around it. The 'Queen' picked up the creature and held it out to me, giving me responsibility to deal with it. I awoke with the strong feeling that I had to do something about the dream. I had known before leaving Britain that Staffy had been diagnosed as having a tumour of the brain, and surmised that I must have been seeing representations of her spirit form and the cancer entity within her physical form. My guess was that she had either died or was in some sort of crisis.
>
> That evening I carried out some healing work. My girlfriend, Angela, 'covered' me with a circle of golden light and I created another circle alongside through which I could send energy via a figure 8 pattern and remain insulated. I called Staffy up in the circle and commanded the entity to separate from her. It did so reluctantly on the third repeat of the order, and began to leap madly around the circle. I asked Anubis' help in putting it into a sleep state and was then able to 'bag' it and send it back to its appropriate dimension using the bow of Artemis. I then carried out some healing with Staffy, replacing the vacuum left by the entity with the Anubis Ray. My intuition at the time was that this work had been necessary to prevent carry-over of the physical condition to other incarnations. I made notes in my diary of the experience. It was the 12th October 1999.

After returning to Britain I had no contact with my friend for several weeks as he had moved to another part of the country. When we got in touch I found him distraught as Staffy had died a few days earlier. He told me that, at what turned out to be the time of my dream, Staffy had become very ill. She had appeared blind and highly distressed, snapping at even those close to her. Her little body would have looked and behaved much as the entity in the dream. Before medical intervention could be sought, however, she had staged a recovery, returning to her old self. She was better for several weeks before quickly deteriorating and being helped by the Vet to pass over.

My comment? A young man who not only knows his occultism, but is also able to effect an exorcism by negotiating time and space. I am delighted that he gave me permission to quote directly from his missive.

Paschat Teachings

I find myself referring once again to a conversation I had with my Paschat friend back in the 1970's on the subject of parallel Universes, the answer he gave when questioned as to the nature of Time, and the fact that there is a point at which all Time exists simultaneously:

> ... Let us say, for example, that a train crashes because an error of judgment has been made, in another, or parallel time dimension those same people will travel on that train, but in that dimension a mistake will not be made and no-one will leave incarnation. Everything is relative to what you are experiencing in any one time-zone and, believe me, you are by no means limited to what you see around you. Equally, you may experience in another time-zone that which appears exactly the same as another in dress, housing, motor cars, customs, and so forth, but with subtle differences. In one you may lose a leg in a crash while in the other, which is fractionally different, you may survive intact. One life may see you rich and enjoying every luxury, another may see you in dire poverty.
>
> 'Mature essence-fragments may elect to enter a time-zone which affords them alternative experiences of the kind that a younger fragment would not be able to handle. Or they may choose to negotiate these during sleep state to test their own strength of mind and rationale.

'Familiarity with present-day conditions, *deja vu*, is simply an indication of existing experiences being lived in another very close or even parallel time-zone. Memory is not limited to the linear past; equally you can remember the future and the present. Dimensions of time often interweave and there are points or warps where the framework between two or more time-zones is fragile. This can give rise to strong imprints from a former period which are commonly known as 'hauntings'. It can also account for missing people who are accidentally projected into another time-zone, but even that constitutes a valid experience for the person in question. The natural structural barriers between bands of time can also be affected by strong emotional impacts, as with localities where suffering or personal shock has taken place.

'All these things will become increasingly apparent to you as your technology advances. Instruments fine enough to perceive subtle changes will open up new territories for the human mind to investigate and conquer. But be sure that you anchor such findings to a sound cosmic philosophy, or you will lose all moral sense and cause yourselves much suffering.

'No doubt some of you are thinking, "but if we can return to any time-zone to re-experience, does it really matter whether we are good or evil?" To the universe, of course, it does not. But to you yourselves, yes, it does! (*The Lion People* Intercosmic messages from the future. pp.26-26. Thoth Publications, first published February 1998. Reprinted. 1989. 1990, 1991, 2001).

A recent advertisement for a well-known make of spectacles featured the eminent scientist Professor Stephen Hawking waxing poetic at the sheer breadth and wonder of the Universe that we see in our night skies, and I found myself saying aloud: 'If only he could see this Universe *from a distance* in its entirety as I have done, and the next one to it, and the one beyond that. You see, they are not all 'black', nor is there a point at which this perpetual stream of cosmic existence begins and ends. Scientists tell us that the Universe, like the Earth, is speeding up, and that there is an unknown and mysterious energy in the Cosmos which issues, or appears to issue, from a vacuum. It defies gravity, and the other three forces known to man - electromagnetism, the strong nuclear force, and the weak nuclear force. This mysterious energy is TIME and Time is *infinite*.

Likewise, Time decrees that the recycling process also continues *ad infinitum*, one Universe continually giving birth to another and so forth. One does not even try to conceive of this process in earthly terms - one simply acknowledges its existence and goes with the flow. There will be 'times' when the cosmic currents appear merciless, and others when they are benign and breathtaking in their sheer beauty. Although I am a Time-Deva, I am still a comparatively young one with much, much more to learn. However, I do know how to negotiate the *speed of time*, although not via the auspices of this frail body.

Reincarnation, dreams, genetic memories, parallel universes - all of these are minor components of Time. When the human race finally comes to realise the power and nature of this, the most profound of all the great Devic Forces, many of its present-day problems will melt into the mists of obscurity. By that time the fragments of the group-soul of *homo sapiens* will have no further need for physical incarnation, having finally ascended to a more exalted dimension, the nature of which will serve to guide them to their next experience in the Halls of Eternity.

CHAPTER 8

THE KINGDOMS OF ELEMENTALS, DEVAS AND ANGLELS

The Four (or Five) Elemental Forces - Eastern and Western Concepts

As the next few chapters of this book will be embracing the deeper aspects of magic and occultism, it behoves us to consider the nature of some of the energies with which the magician or occultist will be working. Since the earliest of times, the realisation dawned upon mankind that going it alone simply wasn't on. Assistance of some kind or other was inevitably required from time to time from powers external to the purely physical, for protection against the elements, fertility in animals, crops, etc., or simply the acknowledgement of some divine force which appeared to wield celestial power over their circumstances, proclivities and destinies. These initial religious efforts were usually directed towards those forces of nature which most affected their lives - fire, air, water and earth. Thus was the basis of all magic conceived.

Those 'acknowledgments' have survived to this present day and age and as I write, the Mother Sun has just cast her first beams across the year 2000, and occultists world-wide will be paying their obeisance to whichever aspects of their respective deities they have elected to acknowledge, love or follow. Have things changed? Never! Every correctly observed Rite involves the invocation of the Four Elements, sometimes simply as guardians of The Four Corners, and at others because they choose to acknowledge these Beings as brothers and sisters rather than forces to be 'commanded' at the pleasure of the magician. However there is one lesson mankind on the whole still has to learn, that being that he/she is not the deciding power in the running of this planet, this universe, or any other celestial body for that matter. It is only by *merging* with these great elemental forces that the peoples of Earth will eventually be allowed to work with them - as brothers and sisters. This leads me into the true nature of The Kingdoms of Deva, and the Spirits of those great elemental forces over which mankind has striven for so many years to control.

First of all, let us effect some essential distinctions, certain parlance common to occult practices tending to render false impressions. There is some confusion of terms when it comes to elementals and *elementary spirits*. In my terms of reference, an elementary spirit is a lesser-evolved entity (miniature field), probably from the sphere of pre-human existence or some time-frequency that has not yet offered it the opportunity for experience in the worlds of matter. I realise that some occultists employ this term when describing thought-forms generated by their use of magical invocations plus will, but I am not, nor ever have been, included in this category. In my understanding (and the light of my personal experience), *elementals* are the spirits of the four elements - add Time, and we have a somewhat heady cocktail!

According to the Western Tradition specific qualities are ascribed to each element. The Salamanders (fire) are associated with creativity, ardour, raw energy, valour and loyalty; the Sylphs with intellectuality, speed, communication, detachment and inventiveness; the Ondines with emotions, feelings, receptivity, understanding and sympathy; and the Gnomes with thrift, acquisition, wealth in all forms, conservation and practicality. Likewise with music and medicine, where Fire is the stimulant, Air the tonic, Water the narcotic, and Earth the sedative. The four 'humours' or psychological types, as outlined by Hippocrates, are also associated with the elements thus: fire - the sanguine, air - the bilious, water - the phlegmatic, earth - the melancholic. Even the Scriptures align them with the four great archangels and their respective beasts: Michael - fire (symbol, the lion), Raphael - air (symbol, the eagle), Gabriel - water (symbol, man) and Uriel - earth (symbol, the bull). So while the priest in his church may invoke in his litanies the assistance of Michael the Archangel, the occultist may be busy with his/her Rite to Gabriel, Uriel or Raphael. Where's the difference?

THE KINGDOMS OF ELEMENTAL, DEVAS AND ANGLES 93

Each Elemental Kingdom has also been accorded a ruler - Djinn being 'King' of the Salamanders, Paralda - 'Queen' of the Sylphs, Necksa - 'Queen' of the ondines and Gob - 'King' of the Gnomes. These names and titles are, of course, purely arbitrary; tradition is simply telling us that all those beings who inhabit these 'Kingdoms' are subject to strict sets of rules, which have to be adhered to by each entity if it is to proceed along its correct evolutionary path.

The elemental forces appear to have featured somewhat differently in certain Eastern conventions, established Indian beliefs, for example, conceiving of three kinds of energy, Vata, Pitta and Kapha, collectively referred to as 'doshas'. As with the Western Tradition, each of these was associated with certain aspects of human behavioural expression: VATA (wind) with the nervous system (Air?), PITTA - with intensity (Fire?), and KAPHA - with matters earthy and practical (Earth?).

The ancient Chinese praxis of Feng Shui (wind, water), which is fast gaining popularity in modern western society, is concerned with the improvement of *ch'i* (energy). This *chi*, however, would appear to be dependent upon five elements - wood, earth, fire, water and metal, which were believed to occur as a result of the interplay between yin and yang. As with yin, yang, and *ch'i*, these five elements were not conceived of as physical substances, but powers or essences describing all matter and attributes. Chinese beliefs associated these elements with time, space, matter, senses, and psychological moods. The element of wood, for example, is assigned to spring, the colour green, and the East. Fire heralds summer, the South and the colour red. Earth, positioned at the centre, is mid-autumn and yellow. Metal is autumn, white, and the West, while Water governs black (the deeper the water the blacker it gets), North, and winter. Full details of this philosophy may found in any book on Feng Shui.

But let us return to the four (five, including time) elements as appropriate to the Western Tradition. During earlier times there were many legends concerning the nature and lives of elemental spirits, one being that, unlike human souls, these spirits of nature were not immortal. However, should one of their kind fall in love and contract a union with a mortal, they could partake of the same immortality as their human lover. This fable is well illustrated in the story of Rusalka, a Water Spirit, which was later featured in the opera of the same name by the Czech composer Antonin Dvorak.

Devic Evolution

Having acquainted my readers with the Elemental Kingdoms, as viewed from both Eastern and Western traditions, where does the term 'deva' enter all this? 'Deva' (Persian *div.* Latin, *divus*), comes from the Sanskrit and should not be confused with the Persian *Daeva* - an evil spirit. Devas featured strongly in the Hindu religion, certain benign deities, notably Indra, being counted among their kind. In recent times, however, it has become commonly used in describing elementals or faery folk generally. Regarding its use in Theosophy, in his *Encyclopaedia of Occultism* the late Lewis Spence defines it thus:

> Devas constitute one of the ranks of orders of spirits who compose the hierarchy which rules the universe under the Deity. Their numbers are vast, and their functions are not all known to mankind, though generally these functions may be said to be connected with the evolution of systems of life. Of Devas there are three kinds -
>
> i) Bodiless Devas
> ii) Form Devas
> iii) Passion Devas
>
> Bodiless Devas belong to the higher mental world; their bodies are composed of Mental Elemental Essence, and they belong to the first Elemental Kingdom.
>
> Form Devas belong to the lower mental world, and while their bodies are composed also of Mental Elemental Essence, they belong to the second Elemental Kingdom.
>
> Passion Devas belong to the astral worlds, and their bodies are composed of Astral Elemental Essence. Devas are creatures superlatively glorious, of vast knowledge and power, calm yet irresistible, and in appearance altogether magnificent.' *(page 122 in the above-mentioned publication).*

While I cannot, in conscience, go along with the latter superlatives, the whole concept does seem to tie in with both Christian and pre-Christian concepts of angelic beings. But taking all this into consideration, why have I seen fit to place myself in the devic category, rather than staying with the 'elemental' tag? There are two main reasons: the first being that the term 'elemental' itself, having magical-cum-occult associations, could render a false impression of the way I function, and, secondly, because the term 'deva' has been applied to me by those in the know, and I was actually introduced as such at a seminar I gave at the Theosophical Society's headquarters in London.

I owe my first knowledge of what are known as 'Angelic Choirs' to my childhood indoctrination into Roman Catholicism, the basic catechism teaching being that there are nine choirs of angels: Seraphim, Cherubim, Thrones, Dominations, Principalities, Powers, Virtues, Archangels and Angels; each having specific duties in the heavenly (or otherwise) scheme of things. This dogma was based on the writing of St.Thomas Aquinas (c1225-1274), who thus earned himself the title 'The Seraphic Doctor' and who was also, albeit on the quiet, an occultist of some distinction, his tutor being the great occultist Albertus Magnus. In fact I spent a good deal of time studying his life and came up with some highly interesting observations, which I presented in lecture form. In addition to information supplied by Magnus, when it came to the study of angelology both men probably owed much to the writings of Dionysus the Areopagite - sometimes known as St.Denis - who lived in the sixth century and was deeply influenced by the Neoplatonic philosopher Proclus (c411-485). Like Proclus, he sought to combine Neoplatonism with Christianity. Dionysus produced four books on the subject of angels: *The Celestial Hierarchy, Ecclesiastical Hierarchy, Divine Names and Mystical Theology.* The angelic theme was taken up later by Hildegard of Bingen (1098-1179), a renowned mystic of her time who was also a skilled writer, poet and musician.

However, angels are by no means the sole property of Catholicism, the scriptural tradition of pre-Christian Judaism featuring as many, if not more. In his *Dictionary of Angels* (Free Press, New York, 1957), Gustav Davidson offers a comprehensive list of angelic nomenclatures, accompanied by descriptions of the specific areas of influence designated to each. The Hebrew for 'angel' is *malak*, while it is actually the Greek *angelos* from which the term *angel* appears to have originated. During certain periods of history, angelology became a serious ecclesiastical and mystical study. In his classic *The Occult Sciences* the eminent Victorian scholar A.E. Waite tells us that in general literature perhaps the most curious work along these lines is Heywood's *Hierarchy of the Blessed Angels*, which he describes as 'a storehouse of curious research'. Other writings he recommends on the subject are *De Apparitionibus Generis Spirituum* by the Jesuit Peter Thyraeus (c1600), *Pneumatologia; or a discourse of Angels, their nature and Office or Ministry* (anon. 1701). Moving into our own times, one of the best books on the subject available at the moment is undoubtedly *The Physics of Angels (Exploring the Realms where Science and Spirit meet)* by Dr. Rupert Sheldrake and Matthew Fox, in which the former describes the Field Theory, as applied to angelic beings, in a way that I could not hope to better.

As I mentioned earlier in this Chapter angels, contrary to Christian tradition, are certainly not born perfect; far from it in fact, as I hope to illustrate, they have, and always will have, free will. Like everything else in this and every other universe, they commenced their life-cycles as what I would describe as miniature fields of energy which, as they expand and accrete, slowly acquire knowledge which in turn results in further field expansion. To put it into simple terms, their evolutionary journey commences as a minute, elemental particle - Fire, Air, Water, Earth or Time. As each elemental field (spirit, if you prefer) evolves, so it becomes aware of, and therefore imbibes the nature and energies of the other four. The process works as follows: a single Time elemental will first of all be drawn to the nature of Fire, since the compatibility between Salamanders and Time beings is very strong. These two elements are not usually comfortable with Earth or Water, so those are likely to be the last two elements to which they attain before they become fivefold or, in other words, a junior angel.

One of the interesting things about the Aquinas angelic divisions is that the Seraphim, Virtues and Powers are believed to be of a Fiery nature; the Thrones and Archangels - Aquatic; The Dominations and Principalities - Aerial; and the Cherubim - Earthy.

(In Ezekiel Satan is described as a Cherubim). In other words, we are back full-cycle to our four elements, to which I have now added number five, which is Time.

Why should this 'new' element suddenly appear on the scene? Is it because hominids are on the verge of recognising, coming to understand, and eventually learning to manipulate that final Element - Time, which in devic terms means that the Higher Powers are ready to pilot the human race into its next evolutionary cycle? Anyway, as I have mentioned earlier, the concept of five elements is hardly new. In certain Eastern countries, for example, the fifth element is known as 'Aether (or Ether)', while prior to 1887 scientists postulated that 'ether' was a very odd invisible and undetectable substance which was 'supported in light and space'. In that year, Americans Mitchelson and Morley reasoned that the movement of the Earth through the 'ether' would necessarily affect the speed of light - that a light ray shining in the direction of the Earth's motions would be travelling 'against the stream' as it were, and be slower than a light ray directed back 'down stream'. However, their experiment showed no difference at all and the ether remained in doubt until Fitzgerald and later Lorentz suggested that objects contract in the direction of motion through the ether - the contraction being precisely the value needed to account for the non-appearance of the anticipated light-velocity differential. A classic case of tailoring the question to fit the answer, there being no such thing as 'ether' in their understanding of the word.

No doubt Professor Stephen Hawking would have knocked such ideas on the head in this day and age, although even *he* is capable of error, as his latest statement that nothing can exceed the speed of light will be disproved when the *speed of Time* is eventually discovered in the years ahead.

To return to the world of the mystic and magi: belief in a five-fold power as far back as the time of Ancient Egypt and before, may be evidenced in the Five Epagomenal Neters and the Ancient Egyptian symbol for the star Sirius, the 'Time-Keeper' for this neck of the galactic woods. There are many more instances of belief in a five-fold energy among the annals of history.

So, while I cannot hope to match the scholarship of those great minds mentioned above, what I can do is to tell the story from the other end of the scale, as a devic Essence who has actually trodden that particular evolutionary path, and thus gained its Five-Fold Nature. I have known what it feels like to exist as a particle without mass, and therefore unattached to the physical - up to a certain point, that is, since no particle remains in one state forever. Everything changes, alternating between the chaotic and stable. The quantum worlds may appear to be chaotic, but rest assured that even within that chaos the seeds of order are surreptitiously ripening. Einstein never accepted the 'chance mode' so often favoured by scientists specialising in quantum physics. In fact he stated 'Quantum mechanics is certainly imposing, but an inner voice tells me it is not the real thing. The theory says a lot, but it does not really bring us any closer to the secret of the "Old One"...' 'God', says Einstein, 'does not play dice'. In other words, there is no such thing as coincidence, in spite of those periods of chaos through which all evolving life-forms must inevitably pass.

One radical difference between the devic kingdoms and the hominid evolutionary pattern is the death syndrome. Not normally possessing solid forms as such, even when their evolutionary journeys take them through the atomic structures of mass, elemental spirits do not 'die'; they simply change by process of accretion. It can be argued that the human field (soul) does likewise, although its body (mass) has a limited span of existence which, once again, is ordained by the physical conditions prevailing on the planet in question.

Angels of Time

So what role, you may ask, does a Time deva play in all this, assuming that it has gained its five-fold nature? Although I am able to enjoy concourse with the planetary and stellar devas my kind are NOT planetary genii. We are the movers and shakers of the Cosmos. Do not think of us in terms of a single unit: we are legion. During our periods of travel we assist other angelic beings in the process of effecting genetic mutations of all kinds, not just on Earth, but in this and every other Universe: and these, too, are multitudinous, but as yet I know them not, being but a child among my kind, with much still to learn and unending tasks to perform. What I can tell my readers, however, is that certain Stellar angelic genii are responsible for the collective evolution of this solar system and all life experiencing therein, *in addition to its parallels in other areas of space-time*. Moreover, this is but one small area of our Universe. Likewise, as mentioned above, there are those angelic beings to whom falls the task of actually creating new universes by producing the appropriate Instanton (the name given by Professor Stephen Hawking and his team to the cone-like particle which contained all the major ingredients essential to the growth and formation of the new universe - matter/gravity, the strong and weak nuclear forces, electromagnetism and Time, the latter being responsible for igniting the 'fuse' which produced the 'Big Bang', or 'singularity', essential to the manifestation of mass at a given frequency). It is with this latter task that the cooperation of the Great Time Entities is needed.

Where Does God Fit In?

I am sure that some of my readers will want to know how devas feel about the subject of God. In my conversations with those planetary genii and senior angels with whom I have been privileged to converse all were in accord, in that their view on supposed 'hot lines to God' was that they were simply not on, such assumptions constituting the sin of pride. While they all agreed that there is a 'single infinite and timeless Source', they felt that calling on it willy-nilly constituted an impertinence generated by pure ego. As to the 'holier-than-thou' approach, may I once again refer to the parable of the Pharisee and the Publican. So, while the proverbial infant may be destined to attain professional achievements *in the fullness of Time*, the ascent to that position cannot be instantaneous (even by the laws of logic and physics), and the Laws of the Creator are nothing if not logical.

Let us return to our angelic friends. Angels, more often than not, are looked upon as being beautiful, benign beings whose only task (aside from providing voices for the heavenly choirs and orchestral players to accompany them) is to guide humans through the dark days of their evolutionary cycle. But hold on a minute - all angels are not on the side of Order. There are also angelic agents of Chaos, or darkness as some might prefer to call it. Take the story of Lucifer, for example. Now there is a classic case for the evidence of free will among the angelic hosts. His sin, we are told, was Pride! Furthermore he was a cherub - which tells us that he commenced his evolutionary cycle as a gnome. Gnomes have always been associated with money ("Gnomes of Zurich") and in my humble capacity as an observer of my own kind, I cannot help but notice the hominid preoccupation with possessions: possessions of money, property, land - each other even! All very Luciferian. There is a legend which speaks of Earth as being a fallen planet and yet Danuih (Gaia) herself is by no means off-track, so from where did this unwelcome devic influence hail, and why are we stuck with it here on Earth?

In 1997 I came across a short article in the *Daily Mail* (12th June), which read as follows:

SISTER PLANET THAT MAY HAVE BEEN PIG-IN-THE-MIDDLE

The Earth may once have had a sister planet which was flung from the solar system, scientists claim. A computer model of the creation of the planets has discovered a 'hole' between the Earth and Mars where a body once existed...'

Looking back over eons of time I can vouch for the accuracy of this claim. However, the planet in question was not ejected from our solar system but still exists therein - *in a lunar capacity!* Its chaotic target is the Earth, but there again it is serving a useful purpose by contributing the chaos/order balance essential to all evolution.

For every deva of Light there is believed to be an angel of darkness. We are back full cycle to the chaos-versus-order scheme of things, and yet both are absolutely essential to the progress of all life, at every level. If we do not learn to cope with the inconsistencies, inconveniences and adversities of chaos, our fields will never expand; or, to use more popularly accepted semantics, our souls will never experience spiritual advancement. Besides, as I have said so many times, chaos is the child of order and order the child of chaos, the excessive build-up of either inevitably exploding into the rebirth of the other. All schools of magic acknowledge the existence of the eternal battle between Light and darkness, good or evil, as, indeed, do all religions. After all, it is all there in the Scriptures and Gospels.

THE KINGDOMS OF ELEMENTAL, DEVAS AND ANGLES

What about fairies, and where do they fit into the devic scheme of things? It would seem that the elemental concept has, over the years, become compartmentalised to the extent that fairies, angels, gnomes, etc. are all viewed as different categories of beings. In fact these are all part and parcel of the Devic Kingdoms. On 5th September 1997 the *Daily Mail* featured the headline: HASN'T EVERYONE SEEN FAIRIES? Among the comments offered by several of those believers who had been interviewed for the article, one sentence from Brian Froud, a fifty-year-old artist and illustrator, caught my eye. It read:

> 'I think angels are grown-up fairies, part of the hierarchy we call supernatural, but it is natural to me. They are the hidden agencies of nature, and the energies underneath it all'.

Congratulations, Mr.Froud. You certainly got it right! This man was also sensible enough to realise that 'wings' usually associated with our devic friends were nothing more than 'the manifestation of energy flowing from their bodies'. After all, at the time when most of these devic essences made their appearance in religious iconography, it was generally believed that wings were the only way anyone (or anything for that matter) could ascend to the heavenly vaults that surround our beautiful, but sadly ill-treated planet. Fairies, gnomes, goblins, trolls; all these are but the nomenclatures allotted to the various denizens of the elemental kingdoms by successive cultures over the ages. Doubtless these have their equivalents in other languages worldwide. Before 'civilisation' and the hardware of its accompanying technology took control of our planet, hominids were much closer to the natural children of Danuih (Gaia). In fact, to this day, in certain isolated country areas, there are still people who put out bowls of milk or other small offerings for the 'fairies', *sidhe*, or 'wee folk'. Animals are much closer to the devic kingdoms than hominids, although there are still those who have carried forward the old ways such as 'horse whispering' (becoming one with the spirit of the animal) and 'talking to the crops'.

Before I forget, there is one other question I am bound to be asked. Of the nine choirs of angels named above, which, if any, represents the element of Time? Take a brief look at the aforementioned elemental categories into which the ancients placed them, and you will notice that there are three Fire (the Seraphim, Virtues and Powers), two Air (the Dominations and Principalities), two Water (the Thrones and Archangels), one Earth (the Cherubim), plus the ninth choir which are simply labelled 'angels', as I learned at school, (which is believed to include what are popularly viewed as Guardian Angels). Now which of the 'Fire Angels' is the odd one out? The Seraphim, of course, with their fiery swords of creation and demolition - these are the Angels of Time, and among their 'juniors' are to be found what the late Dion Fortune so aptly described as 'the occult police'! My autobiography features a poem I wrote when I was in my early twenties. Its title - *The Seraphim.* Should any of my readers be interested in learning more about the nature of Time Devas, I would suggest that they read those lines, as they describe not only the function of these angelic hosts, but also give an insight into their thought-processes.

There will doubtless be those among my readers who will suggest that there are other energy sources, or forces in the universe eager to lend their energies to the aspiring magician, extra-terrestrials for example. I would fully agree, having worked with, and learned much from not only the Eyani, but also other evolved entities from far-flung galaxies. However, the traditional Path is always the safest for the beginner, energies exuded by beings experiencing in any form of mass/matter dissimilar to our own (the Lizard People of the Capella star system in the constellation of Auriga being a prime example) inevitably resulting in problems of a physical (health) nature should the aspirant be incapable of handling their energies.

A final word of advice and, perhaps, warning. There has recently been a flood of DIY books on how to commune with angels, fairies, devas, etc. While these complementary life-forms are always happy to form associations with humankind, *the soul-age of the spirit/ spirits in question, and the level at which one is able to view them, will be dependent upon the soul-age (field band-width) of the human contact, and whether he/she is able to resonate at a particular devic frequency.* To put it in plain English - like inevitably attracts like.

CHAPTER 9

MAGIC/OCCULTISM - THE FACTS BEHIND THE FICTION

Different Magical Systems

The magical package comes in all shapes and sizes, as it has ever done. Open any specialist magazine which covers this and allied subjects and you will see adverts proclaiming magical prowess of all kinds, which can, no doubt, prove very confusing to both beginners and purely interested parties alike. There will be the inevitable cluster of self-termed 'Masters', eager to convince the readers that they and they alone excel in this or that speciality - the Pagan, Greek, Celtic, Norse, Wiccan, Egyptian, Cabbalistic (or Qabalistic, if you prefer), Enochian, Masonic, Eastern or Western Traditions - the list goes on and on so, as the saying goes, 'You pays your money and you takes your pick!'. But does an interest in, or even the practice of any of these systems automatically entitle one to call oneself an occultist? Although some aspirants may be genuinely attracted to, say, Earth Magic, while others are simply carried away by the beauty of a certain Rite, or the feel-good factor experienced in sending kind thoughts and energies to our planet, do such practitioners really understand the principles behind their actions, the real nature of the energies they are invoking, or the level of the periodicity emitted during their ceremonies?

Although there are still those who adhere strictly to the old ritual methods and arcane science as observed by Aleister Crowley, Dion Fortune, and Orders such as those of the Golden Dawn, Silver Star, and Rosicrucians, (whose complicated Ranking Systems I shall shortly be featuring) today's up-and-coming occultists are tending to create their own systems, which is, of course, as it should be. For although the basic principles remain the same, it is only natural that each successive generation should interpret these in the light of the circumstances offered by the 'present'.

According to the old tradition, if faced with a malign force the ritualist would naturally set up a 'banishing rite', which requires all the usual accoutrements, while seemingly ignoring the element of time lost during such a procedure. Why be bothered with such paraphernalia when it is so much easier to use the mind to change the energy level instantaneously (switch to the Ray appropriate to the occasion). Any occultist worth his or her salt would be familiar with the various Rays and their anti-Rays - (compatible/incompatible frequencies in scientific jargon), and therefore be able to issue the appropriate command for the visiting energies to disperse/return to its/their rightful level. This is how the genuine magician would cope. Better still, why not ensure that either one's premises, or the area appropriated for the 'working' are well guarded against intrusion by malign entities in the first place. Should the 'fear' element rear its ugly head, it is also worth bearing in mind that accentuated chaos inevitably reverts to order - a fact that even the laws of physics will substantiate.

Initiation - The Real Facts

As any genuine practitioner of the magical arts will affirm, the early student days can be both horrifying and mentally unnerving to such an extent that many either drop out through sheer fright never to touch the subject again, or run to what they feel to be the safety and shelter of one or other of the well-established religions.

But then genuine initiation bears no resemblance to the academic method of upgrading in that the student will automatically rise to the desired dimension, wherein he/she is faced with a whole new set of problems, difficulties, fears, etc. Handle these and the postulant has succeeded. Fail to cope, and he/she automatically drops back to the position occupied prior to the temporary upgrading. In other words one is offered the power, but if one cannot handle it then it is back to the metaphysical 'drawing board' so to speak. What I am trying to explain is that passing an initiation has nothing whatever to do with learning lines or getting one's metaphysical sums right, but rather the ability to accommodate the energy-level of a more exalted frequency. Fail to effect the necessary adjustment and back one goes to the lower classroom. To put it into metaphysical terms, each 'constant' changes as the periodic cycles increase in speed. The faster the speed (or more exalted the level), the greater the perils on the one hand, but the higher the rewards - in terms of power and the ability to defend oneself, on the other. I shall be dealing with some of the more orthodox occult ranking systems later in this Chapter.

Although in an earlier Chapter I defined the term 'occultism' as I understand and practise it, from what I have seen over the years there would appear to be very few practitioners in the general metaphysical field who actually practise the manipulation of energies external to the purely physical in the way that I described in Chapter 1. But this is little wonder, since most of my occult knowledge and methods have been 'remembered' from my training in the 'Old Country' (Atlantis). However, after effecting a broad scan of today's metaphysical horizon I have been forced to arrive at the following conclusions:

1. That many people who claim occult status are simply fortune-tellers who like the sound of the word, but who haven't a clue when it comes to the real nitty-gritty of the magical arts.
2. There are those who practise occult rituals on a regular basis purely to experience the 'energy high' attained during the Rite. However, since the energies generated by certain rites are often quite powerful, if these are not correctly directed they will naturally find their own point of settlement, which may prove to be an irritant to either the practitioner or the observer.
3. Those 'fireside' occultists who can quote chapter and verse from every book ever written on the subject but, if faced with some real phenomena, wouldn't have a clue as to how to change or disperse an alien energy field (effect an appropriate exorcism).
4. Those who dress up in fancy clothes, Ancient Egyptian, Greek, Norse, Celtic, or whatever, and prance around in ballet-like fashion in the (often sincere!) belief that they are practising magic! I have even heard of some in this category

who actually invite the general public in to witness the display - for a charge, naturally! Of course it can be argued that one does not need to be an occultist, or even a student of the metaphysical arts, to enjoy attending a Rite. Fair enough, as long as the 'spectator mode' is viewed in that context only. But having been frequently called on to adjust numerous 'psychological damages' effected by either the the inability of the observer to absorb the energies generated, or the ignorance of the Hierophant as to the real nature of what he/she has actually invoked, I do feel that an element of caution should always be adopted in such proceedings. If you want to worship the Old Gods, relax and have a lot of fun in the process, then so well and good. But please don't feel the need to assume the title of 'occultist', Master, or whatever, in order to make what you hope will be a good impression.

5. Members of those 'Secret Occult Lodges' which can prove a trap in that they frequently attract the egotist intent upon pursuing the Leadership role. Personality clashes are therefore a foregone conclusion when the energies start to rise. As for the subject of 'Secret Occult Societies', I shall have a cautionary tale to tell in a later Chapter.
6. The loner who works straight from the mind without need of bell, book and candle, and who can switch traditions according to the demands of the moment - in my book of rules this is the real occultist.

Any fringe dabbler may call him/herself an occultist but in the final analysis the proof of the pudding is inevitably in the eating.

The 'Lodge' System

This system, which is still kept alive in Freemasonry, was much favoured by occultists in the past and is still staunchly upheld by those who elect to ignore the winds of change. The various criteria required for acceptance into a Lodge naturally varied according to Lodge rules, in some cases those accepted being given a special 'Lodge Name' by which they were known while within those hallowed precincts. The names chosen were often those of ancient god-forms, and thus varied according to Lodge tradition. As there is already a wealth of literature available on this and allied subjects, it behoves me to bow out at this point.

Path Workings

I would describe Path Workings as a psychological technique much favoured by certain occultists as a method of alerting the conscious mind to traditions of the past, while also encouraging the student to broaden his/her awareness via the mental process of imagery and creative imagination.

These techniques feature a series of guided mental journeys during which the student is confronted with symbolic scenes and archetypal images which are designed to help the psyche to understand, and therefore learn to negotiate, the more metaphysical concepts and situations with which it will inevitably be faced should it elect to proceed along the occult path. Pathworkings can also serve as a mental discipline for the serious aspirant, especially in the early stages of both psychic development and occult study. Its limitations, however, lie in the fact that it deals essentially with the past, and therefore with known and tested psychological responses and magical archetypes. However, the real magician is, by nature, a time-traveller and therefore just as concerned with the future and what that is likely to bring, while also aspiring to understand and negotiate the energies of worlds way beyond the paradigms of this Universe.

This is not a system which I myself use, its limitations for a Time Deva being very obvious. I am, however, given to understand that it is popular with beginners and those who, although interested in matters occult, have no serious intention of proceeding into deeper magical waters.

Magic and Money

'Magic is NOT a profession'; wrote The Abbe Alphonse-Louis Constant, (1810-1875), better known by the Qabalistic name he chose to adopt - Eliphas Levi - and one of the most celebrated occultists of his time. Would that those in this day and age who call themselves occultists, and charge exorbitantly high fees for their questionable services, would heed the words of this Master. It will doubtless be argued that although Levi was highly acknowledged in the magical field, there were rumours that he reaffirmed his allegiance to Catholicism on his deathbed. Such stories have, however, since been regarded by many as nothing more than Catholic justification for their belief in the ultimate superiority of their creed.

However, genuine tutorials, be they for psychism or occultism, often require the expenditure of energy on behalf of the teacher and, perhaps, the cost of premises for the use thereof, including light refreshments. Since money is, after all, a form of energy, then an appropriate fee is in order. It is only when the big EGO enters the scene, and the 'necessity' becomes the 'exorbitant', that the Scales of Maat take over and Thoth writes in his Book.

One of the earliest tasks I was given to undertake when I first set foot on the occult path was to learn and understand the Nine Occult Laws. How many of those purporting to be occultists in this day and age have ever heard of these? So how could they comprehend their message, or be conversant with their meanings at all levels? Perhaps this would be an appropriate point in my narrative at which to introduce them, so that they may serve as guidelines for the interpretation of any more complicated magical issues I may feel inclined to include in the forthcoming pages:

The Nine Metaphysical (Cosmic) Laws

1. THE LAW OF REBOUND

This Law designates that a superior force will always cause a lesser power to recoil. To put this into more personal terms, if one comes up against another person, or a disembodied energy field that is stronger than one's own, whatever one projects in its direction will be returned PLUS the full force of the Rebounder.

2. THE LAW OF THREE REQUESTS

Rather more metaphysical, this one, in that it suggests that all requests which involve major decisions, be they related to matters material, psychological, or issuing from the subtle dimensions of non-locality, should be repeated in triplicate. The reason for this? The first utterance alerts the conscious mind, the repeat engages the reasoning faculty while the third statement is believed to make direct contact with the psyche or field (as illustrated in the Biblical story of Peter's denial).

3. THE LAW OF CHALLENGE

All visions, dreams, sources of information, suspicions, anything, in fact, that would appear to issue from beyond the bounds of rational, logical thinking should be challenged. The lesson here is one of absolute honesty, as one should always be aware of the subtle line that divides present reality from interpenetrative alien frequencies, and inspiration from delusion, ecstasy and frenzy being but a hair's breadth apart.

4. THE LAW OF EQUALITIES

When two equal forces meet one will eventually give way to the other, which then rises in status (increases field band-width or gathers mass?) This Law is re-echoed in the natural laws of science and may be clearly evidenced in particle physics.

5. THE LAW OF BALANCE OR EQUIPOISE

This Law designates that everything should function according to its relevant frequency or at its correct level. For example, sitting for hours round a table trying to drum up sufficient PK to move it six inches, when the same effect can be produced by giving it a slight push, is both a fruitless task and a case of misplaced energy. The Law of Balance is also concerned with the state of equipoise necessary for the satisfactory functioning and correct expression of energy at any level, which relates it particularly to the field of disease and healing. It denounces excesses of any kind and demands, for example, that the physical body be treated with courtesy because it is host to many other life-forms including the four Elements, without whose kind offices there would be no molecular structure and therefore no manifestation of physical form in the first place.

6. THE LAW OF SUMMONS

Another more metaphysical (or parapsychological, perhaps?) Law, which designates how things do or do not respond to one's wishes. If, therefore, one makes a particular request, be it at any level, only to find that the response is either incorrect or disappointing, the fault may well lie within oneself. Either one is exceeding one's personal powers or requesting 'dues' to which one is not entitled. Such imposed limitations should not be blamed on so-termed 'superior forces' of either good or evil, as they may well originate in either the cerebral workings or the psychology of the person concerned. There is plenty of medical evidence to suggest that when we want something badly, the brain actually goes into reverse and emits energies that either block or repel it. However, for the benefit of those among us whose paths have led us into non-local territories (other dimensions beyond the purely physical), this Law has more meaningful connotations, especially in the realms of exorcism or the dispersion of negative force-fields.

7. THE LAW OF POLARITIES

Positive/negative, anima/animus, masculine/feminine, active/passive/ yin/yang - the process of individuation both rational and field-wise - all these are expressions of this Law. We need to be well polarized within ourselves before we can tread the inter-Cosmic paths or, if you prefer, access the Cosmic Super-Highway. In faster frequencies polarity distinctions become blurred, the two aspects eventually blending into the One - the Androgyne. We are advised that at the human race's present stage of evolution the ideal state is for the anima and animus to be in perfect balance within the individual, neither obtruding nor breaking cosmic law. But how many of us are perfect? The answer is, of course, NONE!

8. THE LAW OF CAUSE AND EFFECT

Commonly referred to among arcane teachings as The Law of Karma. Karma is strictly an Eastern term although, as has previously been explained, it is loosely used by many people to express the 'as ye sow so shall ye reap' principle. A generally unheeded aspect of this Law involves the exchange of energies, meaning that we should never expect anything for nothing, although the reciprocation need not always be in 'kind'. For example, a poor person receiving a gift of money need not repay in cash, but could render a service to the giver that is appropriate to their means and talents. Conversely the rich person, who inherits money he/she has not laboured to obtain, should consider the acquisition as Karmic and dispense his/her largesse accordingly.

9. THE LAW OF ABUNDANCE

(sometimes referred to as the Law of Opulence). This Law expresses the attraction of like for like, e.g. money makes money, a fear is an unrequited wish, etc. My old Nanny used to have an appropriate saying, 'show me your friends and I'll tell you what you are'. As it was associated with non-conservation, in olden days it was referred to as 'The Miser's Dread'. When one is down to one's last penny or pound one is advised to go out and spend it, for an energy spent attracts a similar energy. I have frequently given away something I valued to a friend whose need I deemed greater than mine, only to find an article of similar type or value presented to me shortly afterwards. There is, however, a difference between throwing one's money away chaotically and expecting others to foot the bill, and being genuinely in need through no fault of one's own. I often hear it said among esotericists that 'the Universe will provide'. I can assure my readers that she does, but only if one deserves it!

Although in the aforegoing I have tended to simplify matters by emphasizing the effects of these precepts on the individual, I do assure my readers that they can be applied to all levels of experience. How much of their message we choose to understand, or are willing to apply, will, however, be decided by such considerations as to whether we are sufficiently open-minded to accord their possibilities an honest consideration, whether or not we have individuated from the hominid collective, and the band-width of our fields (soul-age).

Occultism and Science

There is what I feel to be an unhealthy prejudice among some psychics and so-termed occultists against those followers of the paranormal whose interests or professions either border on, or are actually involved with the sciences. On one occasion, when lecturing in the Southern Counties, I was stopped in my tracks by a man in the audience who declared in rather loud tones, 'The trouble with you scientific types is that you come into our world, with all your fancy terms, and before you've been in it five minutes you are telling us all what to do'. My rejoinder? 'Well, tell me sir, how long have you yourself been into this line of study?' He replied - 'My wife and I have been into this sort of thing for five years, so put that in your pipe and smoke it!' 'Try fifty-five', I rejoined. After a moment's silence he and his companion arose and left!

What I told him was perfectly true, and anyone who has either the time or patience to read my autobiography will note that my serious studies of the magical arts commenced when I was about fifteen, although my psychic gifts were in evidence almost from the time I was born, as my Nanny, were she still in incarnation, would be only too willing to attest to. But in view of the scientific origins of occultism, why the present-day anti-science stance?

Even a cursory glance at the history of magic will serve to show that science and occultism were once part and parcel of the same scientific package. All the great occultists of the past were scientists. These were the alchemists who pursued the theory and practice of the Magnum Opus, the philosopher's stone, or the concept of converting base metal into gold which, taken in its true metaphysical concept, referred not to the material substance, but to the refining of the spirit. Geber, Rhasis, Morien, Albertus Magnus, Thomas Aquinas, Alain of Lisle, Raymond Lully, Nicholas Flamel, Isaac of Holland, Bernard Trevisan, Thomas Norton, Thomas Dalton, Sir George Ripley, Paracelsus, Denis Zachaire, Thomas Charnock, Berigard of Pisa, John Dee, Henry Kunrath, Jacob Boehme, J.B. Van Helmont, Butler, Alexander Sethon, Eirenaeus Philalethes, John Frederick Helvetius - one could go on.

Occultism has also played its part in the history of our Isles, the Spanish Armada episode being a typical example. Drake's insistence upon finishing his game of bowls was not, it would seem, due to his preoccupation with the game, but because Queen Elizabeth's personal occultist/astrologer, Dr.John Dee, had divined horoscopically the exact time of the Armada's arrival! It was rumoured that Elizabeth herself was a member of an elite Occult Lodge which also included Lord Stanley, Mary Stanley and Dr. John Dee among its members.

I have before me the current Directory of Members for the Scientific and Medical Network, of which I myself am also a member. It would take several lines of my WP's print to accommodate the academic qualifications of some of these brilliant men and women. And yet, included in the summary of their successes (and, in many cases, their services to mankind), are their interests in healing, psychism, spirituality, and the paranormal in all its forms.

Nor are these 'interests' purely academic - most of the people named actually practise in one or other field of healing, psychism or metaphysics. Do things ever change? I think not.

As for my own stance in the scientific-cum-magic debate, frankly, I find the terminology of science infinitely more suited to the expression of what I already know, and what I am still learning, than the oft-times offensive jargon used by both psychics and lay-folk alike. When questioned regarding my metaphysical interests I have often met with such retorts as, 'Oh, you're a fortune teller, then', 'Isn't that all witchcraft stuff?', 'Have you had treatment for it?'; 'Didn't anyone tell you that Black Magic is evil, and that God will punish you for your sins?' Nor have such remarks necessarily issued from the lesser educated who, surprisingly enough, are often highly sympathetic towards the paranormal. However, employ the terminology of quantum mechanics, nuclear physics, medicine, psychology, genetics or neuroscience in replying to their questions and the reception is somewhat different, and decidedly more respectful, in spite of the fact that one is saying exactly the same thing. So, as I see it, the sooner we discard the old 'bogeys' the better, and while there are still those scientists (technologists, in many cases) who choose to pooh-pooh anything even vaguely connected with the paranormal, there are just as many (more, in fact) among those of their disciplines, who both think and feel otherwise. Occultism is, after all, an exact science in that it deals with the nature, understanding and manipulation of energies external to the purely physical. But tell that to some practitioners who claim metaphysical prowess and the response is a blank stare.

Occult Ranking Systems

On the next page is an example of a ranking system which incorporated three famous Occult Orders of the past: The Order of the Golden Dawn, The Order of the Rosy Cross, and The Order of the Silver Star. Note how the Sephiroth of the Qabalistic tree have been appropriated to each rank. While I am not a Qabalist myself, nor ever have been, that system being too 'hominid orientated' for this old deva, I can follow the sequence quite easily. However, having discussed it with one or two occultists of note in the past, I was amazed to discover that none of them really understood the link

Grades

Sephiroth	Grade	Equation
-	Neophyte	0 = 0
Malkuth	Zelator	1 = 10
Yesod	Theoricus	2 = 9
Hod	Practicus	3 = 8
Netzach	Philosophus	4 = 7
Tiphareth	Adeptus Minor	5 = 6
Geburah	Adeptus Major	6 = 5
Chesed	Adeptus Exemptus	7 = 4
Binah	Magister Templi	8 = 3
Chokmah	Magus	9 = 2
Kether	Ipsissimus	10 = 1

between Adeptus Exemptus and Magister Templi, which is usually referred to as 'Babe of the Abyss' (the need to be spiritually reborn before one can ascend to the rank of Magister Templi). Pan is often referred to as the link in this extraordinary chain, but none of the occultists with whom I have discussed this seem to know why. Well, for those interested, here is the answer. Pan is one of the great Earth Devas, to whom falls the responsibility for the evolution of all growing things. He is the Consort of the Planetary Genius we call Gaia (Danuih to me and mine!), and it is these two great devas who, together, are involved with the growth and development of the species known as *Homo Sapiens*. In order for the magician to sever the link which binds him/her to the hominid collective, he/she needs to be reborn from the womb of Pan, to individuate from the hominid collective, thus acknowledging and being able to communicate and work with ALL LIFE both in this world/Universe, and many, many others.

CHAPTER 10

RITUAL - FACTS, FANTASIES AND THE FEEL-GOOD FACTOR

The Nature and History of The Rite - A Psychological Analysis

Occultists come in 'all shapes and sizes', each appearing to be drawn to some specialised area of metaphysics. So it is with your author only, instead of adhering to the usual path of ceremony and Lodge, my way is via the explanation of this and myriad other Universes; a Path which is, after all, more natural to a Time Deva. Nevertheless, my years on Earth in the Observer Mode have served to alert me to the true nature of the hominid soul (field), and, given time, its ultimate cosmic achievements. After all, this Universe is simply a body and, just as the bacteria in our gut view our brains as their 'god' (we can either treat them well or abuse them!), so we, our solar system, etc. are the bacteria in the gut of the galaxy, and ditto the galaxy to the Universe, and this Universe to the next, ad infinitum. The whole picture - well, as much as I, or others of my kind are able to perceive - reminds me somewhat of Russian dolls, in that at one end of the scale particles appear to become smaller and smaller, while at the opposite end, infinity stretches forth its relentless challenge to our consciousness and, of course, our evolution. And yet, the smallest is contained within that infinity, wherein it constantly adds to the growth of its 'parent'.

I must refrain from adopting too devic an approach and concern myself more with the planet upon which a fragment of my field is employed to 'observe', and thus observing both add to my own field-data-banks, and pass as much information as I can on to anyone here on this planet who might be ready to comprehend it. So, let us effect an analysis of the practice favoured by so many humans, that of Ritual. In my book *The Psychology of Ritual*, I have dealt with this subject in depth, from all viewpoints including the psychological and medical. Anyone interested in the deeper aspects of the Rite is therefore referred to this work. However, I intend to borrow a few excerpts from my earlier text, which might, hopefully, serve to throw some light onto the power and influence of the Rite, both in specialised fields such as religion and magic, and in ordinary, everyday life.

Evidence of the Rite has come down to us from the earliest records, and if we are to lend credence to oral and metaphysical traditions, it was in existence long before the pages of recorded history. Rites, however, cover a multitude of purposes and carry a variety of messages, as we shall see. It should also be borne in mind that in those very early days, magic and religion were synonymous, so that which might appear as impious mumbo-jumbo to the modern religious thinker was highly respected and devotional to the participants of the time.

Some categorization will, no doubt, make it easier for the reader to gain a clearer perspective of the nature of, and intention behind, some of the more familiar rites that we take so much for granted, as well as the lesser known rituals which this work has not the space to accommodate. Here, then, is a list which I feel to be fairly comprehensive:

1. Recollective ceremonies - the remnants of rites of earlier, more advanced civilizations, the origins and true meanings of which have become obscured.
2. The worship, or acknowledgement of cosmological or celestial influences - the sun, moon, stars, or natural phenomena such as thunder, lightning, and so on.
3. Pantheistic, Pagan and Animistic Rites (animism being the belief that all inanimate objects and natural phenomena have a living soul or essence) in which due deference is paid to the spirits of nature. Seasonal rituals would come under this category, also the rites of sympathetic magic (invocation or evocation through mimicry).
4. Placatory or Propitiatory Rites - performed with a view to keeping the gods or spirits happy so that they do not give

vent to their wrath at the population's expense.
5. Ancestral Rites - which involve making contact with, and securing the good offices of, those of the tribe who have passed on.
6. Self-exploratory Rites - including those self-analysis techniques which project the participant back into his or her own inner resources.
7. Fertility Rites - involving the multiplication principle which, as much as it may surprise some, is not limited to the human reproductory system.
8. Social Rites - including those Rites which greet us when we first enter life, Maturation and Puberty Rites which are designed to prepare the young people of the tribe for the step into adult life, and the Last Rites administered at the time of death.
9. Sacrificial or expiatory Rites - which make their appearance in both religion and magic to this very day.
10. Initiatory Rites - including Rites of Submission, many of which originally involved physical mortification or deprivation. In this day and age, however, as with many other rites which originated in more primitive times, these are usually enacted symbolically.
11. Supplicatory Rites - including general unspecified collective prayer offerings and invocations which may or may not involve energy exchanges (gifts). These can be purely devotional, or they may include specific pleas for bounty or guidance.
12. Rites of Protection, Purification, Banishment, Cleansing and Healing - which naturally vary in intention according to the persuasion of the users.

Most rites, however, are a blend of several of the above categories. For example, they nearly all include a devotional acknowledgement and/or a request of some kind. Although they may not have started off that way, accumulated layers have frequently been added to accommodate the faiths of conquering nations and/or the tenets of new religions or ideologies.

The above categories can also be subdivided as follows:

a) Public Rites, in which anyone can take part although the quality of the energy generated will obviously affect each participant in a slightly different way.
b) The Solitary or Personal Rite, which can be performed by the lone individual within his or her own space.
c) The Secret Rites of 'closed' groups or collectives.
d) Simple Rites that carry no great mystique, which can be safely executed by anyone.

The latter category obviously raises the question as to whether there are rites which are not safe for participation by all. The answer must be 'yes'. The psychology behind this will, I trust, become obvious as this Chapter progresses.

There are also five basic codes via which the rite may be approached, each of which emphasizes a particular area of human psychology (and the human brain!):

1. *The Severity Code* - which features in Teutonic Magic, the martial arts, warrior and heroic rites, certain African and Amerindian rituals and the harsher Christian and Islamic practices - is of a disciplinary and sometimes punitive nature, and can involve physical mortification which may vary in intensity according to the tradition of the tribe or ethos concerned.
2. *The Emotional Code* - frequently associated with the Celtic, romantic or eco-system of magic, reaches deeply into the feeling nature and can therefore be abreactive (inducing the release of repressed emotion). If handled in a balanced manner, however, it can supply a subconscious outlet in an otherwise emotionally arid existence.
3. *The Contemplative Code* - with its strongly mystical and ascetic undertones, is to be evidenced in the Far Eastern observances, as well as in certain Christian practices.
4. *The Intellectual or Analytical Code* - often associated with Qabalism and the Western Hermetic Tradition.
5. *The Instinctive Code* - as practised in primitive tribal rituals, sympathetic magic, pagan and animistic traditions and certain branches of Wicca.

These can be classified as 'introversial' or 'extroversial', according to the overt or covert nature of the rite on the one hand, or the psychological effect it has on the participants on the other.

Some public rites may appear to involve more than one code, the Catholic Mass, for example, is a Sacrificial Rite which frequently carries an intellectual content for the clergy and an emotional one for the laity. In essence, however, it qualifies as 'Intellectual' because its content is carefully planned and rigidly adhered to.

Active/passive, patrist/matrist/ animus/anima, categories can also be applied as follows:

1. *The Severity Code* - introverted, covert, active, patrist and of animus emphasis.
2. *The Emotional Code* - extroverted, overt, passive, matrist, and of anima emphasis.
3. *The Contemplative Code* - introverted, covert, passive, patrist and of an anima emphasis.
4. *The Intellectual Code* - introverted, covert, passive, patrist and of animus emphasis.
5. *The Instinctive Code* - extroverted, overt, active, matrist and can be of either anima or animus emphasis.

When dealing with the individual psyche, however, one should remember that these are but generalizations, as an actively inclined patrist might, on certain occasions, choose to involve him or herself in a more submissive rite. However, the overall code will prevail, those taking part becoming caught up in the essential nature of the ceremony.

So much for the technical side. I am sure that this being essentially a metaphysical book, what my readers really want to know about are those magical rituals which always seem to be lurking in the background, the energies emitted by such rites, and how they affect any individual who may see fit to attend one such ceremony.

As I have mentioned previously, although I am not a ritualist by nature, my training as an occultist has obliged me to participate in a certain amount of liturgy as part of my tutorials although, in truth, I have never felt really comfortable in any of the prescribed roles of ceremonial magic. Occasionally I have fleeting memories of certain rites which were enacted during my life as a Paschat

(Eyani), which reduce me to tears to this day - tears of love, warmth, and a complete oneness of a kind that I have never, as yet, experienced on this planet, Earth. I naturally share similar feelings of 'belonging' with my own devic kind, 'emotions', (if you could call them such) for which there are no adequate words of description in the context of hominid understanding.

Emotional rituals in particular would seem to be essentially hominid practices, which makes sense in that the emotional element, which dominates many rites, is in keeping with the watery nature of the hominid species. Surveying society as it is today, however, ritual in daily existence does appear to have become essential to survival in this modern world.

The Sacred Instrments of Magical Ritual

All genuine occult-cum-magical rites involve the use of four sacred instruments, each of which is associated with one of the four elements, and according to some rites, used to 'command' the presence/protection of the elemental four. Fire is traditionally commanded by the Wand; Air by the Sword; Water by the Chalice or Cauldron, and Earth by the Pentacles. However, an occultist may vary these according to the customs of his/her tradition. In my own practices, for example, I prefer to use the Sistrum for Fire; the Winged Disc for Air, a Silver Cup containing distilled or pure mineral water for Water, and the Mirror of Hathor for Earth. These instruments also correspond with the 'four corners' in that Fire, the senior element, is always invoked from the South, Air from the East, Water from the West and Earth from the North. One is often asked what happens in other parts of the globe, Australia, for example. Since we are dealing with principles rather than actual locations it matters very little, and the Hierophant is always recommended to adhere to the traditional approach which has been tried and tested for safety over many, many centuries.

Setting Up a Rite

As I have explained, Rites come in all shapes, sizes and systems, so to speak, from those Masonic Rites usually associated with the males of the species to the more popular Earth Rites, the adherents of which, in this day and age, seem only too happy to perform for the public media. I have watched one or two of these on television and was happy to note that, as far as the conjuration of the elemental forces was concerned, the Wiccans, at least, were careful to observe the old ways.

On the rare occasions when I have set up and performed a Rite, it has usually been at the request of either a specific group or some student of the occult anxious to both learn his/her trade on the one hand, or to observe the effects of the Rite on the atmosphere on the other, while also bearing in mind that all Rites should carry one important factor - INTENTION. In other words, one should not partake in a Rite purely for one's own pleasure, but utilise the energy generated for some useful, loving or caring purpose. On one occasion when I was requested to perform a Rite for the Earth, a well-known and highly respected scientist was present in the 'observation' mode, complete with appropriate instruments which would register any changes in atmosphere, electrical frequencies, etc. Having positioned those suitably qualified at the Four Corners (North, South, East and West), I issued the appropriate requests to the elemental forces for their assistance, love and enlightenment, after which the energies in the room commenced to build up rapidly. I won't bore my readers with the intricate details of the Rite, but suffice it to say that we achieved the desired result.

When a Rite is completed, there is a special way of closing down which I am always careful to observe. This involves once again facing to the four points of the compass in turn, thanking the elemental forces for their presence and assistance, and asking them politely (I never command!) to return to their relevant areas in space/time. The Rite is then closed down and the space occupied thoroughly cleansed. As an occultist I obviously have a special 'Ray' which is permeated throughout my abode, and this is always strengthened and re-energised following the use of my premises for a Rite of any kind. In case my readers might be interested in the 'technical' results of my friendly scientist's observation, the needle on his instrument went 'way over the top'. In other words we were working with energies which, in the electromagnetic spectrum anyway, were well above the normal. Such energies do, of course, affect the human brain, and sometimes adversely as we shall see when I come to the final Chapter tin his book. So, if you are uncomfortable with power lines, X-rays, or radioactivity of any kind, steer clear of the higher frequencies of the Devic Ray or you could, as a certain practitioner of the Dark Arts discovered to his dismay, end up hairless!

On the odd occasion when obliged to effect a Public Rite, I have always created a 'sealed energy field' within which to operate, which I dissolve after the Rite is over. There is one, most important principle that I always adhere to when engaging in the employment of energies from other dimensions - NEVER LEAVE A VACUUM. In other words, always close the door or, as the gospel explains, 'Shall not seven more enter'. And never does this principle apply more than in the practise of exorcism, as I shall be explaining shortly.

Readers may note that I am constantly emphasising the fact that one should never command that which is more powerful than oneself, for obvious reasons if you think about it, the elemental forces being infinitely more mighty than those who seek their aid. This has resulted in neophytes questioning me as to how one can attract the elemental forces into one's Rite without actually ordering them to attend? Easy. I refer any such querents to Chapter 3 of this book, under the heading REMOTE VIEWING, and the story of Dr.Barbara McClintock. This eminent scientist and Nobel Prize winner effected her 'entry' into the consciousness of the substances with which she was working by BLENDING AND BECOMING ONE WITH THEM. Only in this way will the student ever really come to know and understand the Devic Forces, and be permitted a degree of access to their field databanks, thus availing him/herself of at least some tiny fraction of their cosmic knowledge.

Taken overall, there is an endless catalogue of magical procedures for the student to experiment with, all of which can be easily dispensed with if the aspirant is prepared to use his/her mind rather than relying on methods which are more appropriate to the age which heralded their inception. Here is a prophecy for the future: during this new millennium the evolution of the human soma will undergo a quantum leap following changes in the DNA of all species extant on this planet. Virtual Reality will then dispense with ritual once and for all.

A quick word of advice on the positive/negative issue: there is a point in the evolution of all species at which these two apparently opposing factions of the Law of Polarity finally blend into the one - the Androgyne. But as things are here at present, that point is way over the top of the scales of all known measurements, from the magical to the scientific, so my advice to all aspirants, regardless of their sexual inclinations, is to decide who is 'outgoing' and who is 'receptive', and take it from there.

'Black' Magic

One so often hears of this or that group being caught practising the 'black arts', which prompts many decent and mentally disciplined people to place such abhorrent practices under the general canopy of magic. The late A.E. Waite described Black Magic as 'The perversion of a legitimate mystic science'. Just as there are angels of Light, so there is also the belief that these radiant Beings have their counterparts in the world of Darkness. In other words, what we are facing is the Order-Chaos principle, which is inevitably interpreted in the light of the beliefs of the time. I very much doubt whether rites carried out by drug-sodden, sexual perverts, of the kind so often featured in certain areas of the popular press, actually carry much power, apart from that of their own inevitable destruction, hence the saying that 'the Devil always comes to collect His own'. In this day and age we may not acknowledge the legions of Beelzebub as outlined in, say, the Grimorium Verum, the Grand Grimoire, or the Grimoire of Pope Honorius, but there are doubtless their equivalent in modern society, albeit conveniently coached in politically correct terms.

Much of the kind of Black Magic featured in novels by the late Dennis Wheatley, for example, was based on ancient demonic rites which relied upon the practitioner's belief in the existence of a Satanic character with an army of demons available to perform at his beck and call. As a Deva I obviously do not share this primitive-cum-medieval picture of a kind of pantomime demon-king, although I do acknowledge the forces of chaos which, in their destructive mode, are capable of wreaking havoc in the lives of many. However, chaos also has its constructive side in that it can rid us of the dead wood in both our personalities and everyday life. In the final analysis evil, whether it manifests via perversion, cruelty or the defiling of accepted ways of behaviour, inevitably leaves a path of destruction in its wake. But then humanity has the free will to choose and, having effected that choice, must pay the price somewhere along the cosmic line of Time.

Ritual in Contemporary Religious Practices

Some years ago I engaged in correspondence with an eminent scientist who was studying the effect of ritual on the human psyche. His first letter commenced as follows:

> As a scientist I am presently exploring the metaphysical and spiritual aspects of personal and corporate worship - its nature, meaning and purpose. I am also attempting to formulate a scientific approach to an understanding of the dynamics of 'energies' generated by personal and corporate devotions in the course of the church ceremonial, and the control and direction of these 'energies' by the priest, in service of the Divine.

My reply, which was dated 1st April 1993, read as follows:

> You ask how the Hierophant uses energies generated to manipulate the minds of those present. It is my opinion that, in most cases, this manipulation is not effected consciously, but rather by the continued insertion of emphasis on the dogmas of the religion in question. In other words, once people enter an ecstatic (or even a semi-frenzied) state, left-hemisphere logic is overpowered by instinctive (NOT intuitive) emotionalism, (hominids being easily manipulated via the emotional factor), which makes for fertile ground for the planting (or nurturing) of the seeds of the faith or ideal in question.

Dehumanisation is the name given to the psychological process that takes place when a crowd or gathering of people assumes a group identity. This may be witnessed in witch-hunts, lynch mobs, unruly sports gatherings and incidents of emotionally or fear-induced mass hysteria. In his essay 'The Nature of Crowds' the distinguished author and scientist Dr. Lyall Watson commenting on the views of the neglected writer Elias Canetti, states:

> Canetti regards the crowd as an organism in its own right. At one moment the street is empty save for a random scattering of individuals, and in the next, in response to a mysterious signal,

there is a concerted action. People push together to form the nucleus of a crowd. Those involved in the action seldom know what has happened. If stopped and questioned they are unable to provide any reasonable reply.

One also, one has to consider the Group Shadow, which inevitably rises from the union of minds alongside any more exalted energy fields that may be decreed by the overall soul-age of the group concerned. Should the Shadow take preference, the Hierophant himself may well be used as a programming agent for less desirable cosmic elements.

Sometimes a particular priest or church dignitary appears to exude a powerful, charismatic effect over people. I make no claim to being in the 'know' in such matters but as I see it, such persons generate, or are generated by, specific energy fields which can have the effect of inducing ASC's (altered stated of consciousness) in their followers, even during the course of normal conversation.

The letter then went on for several more pages, and involved technical terms which I do not feel to be appropriate in a book of this kind. However, we did eventually get onto the subject of the Catholic Tridentine Mass, the structure of which is viewed by many experts in such matters as being somewhat 'special', since it contains many of the ingredients that were considered by the ancients to constitute the perfect Rite. The author, Furze Morrish, who considered himself something of an expert in such matters, commented to this effect in his book *The Ritual of Higher Magic*. The *Lavabis me* (I will wash my hands), is a typical example, when the Priest dips his fingers in the water to indicate a cleansing of both body and spirit. This simple rite preceded all the great rituals of ancient times, as did the Confiteor - the Celebrant's 'confession of sins' - in order to meet with the state of purity required for communication with the gods. The Gloria which follows on, constitutes a paean of praise in the manner observed in many pre-Christian faiths, while the *Munda cor meum* represents a typical celebrant's invocation for access to more exalted frequencies.

The Canon of the Mass, which includes the Consecration of the Bread and Wine which are being prepared for Transubstantiation - the point which it is believed that the actual essences (fields) vacate the substances which are then taken over by the body and blood of

Christ. Unknown to many people, transubstantiation is nothing new. In the ancient Greek Epoptai, the sacred ears of corn were believed to be transubstantiated into the Essence of the Goddess Demeter!

One could go on, but there has to be a point at which I must stop since the Mass itself, in its original Tridentine Latin Form is a Rite deserving pages and pages of psychological, neuroscientific and magical analysis, more, I fear, than this book could accommodate in a single Chapter. Suffice it to say that the Rituals of the major Religions, from the High Latin of the old Catholic Mass to the happy-clappy alleluias of today's more 'liberal' services, are just as much Rites as those magical practices which are undertaken in all sincerity by those who fervently believe this to be the way to make contact with both their higher selves, and energies from more exalted universal frequencies, with (we hope) the best possible intentions.

In my book *The Psychology of Ritual* I have given examples of Rites worldwide, from the most primitive to those favoured by modern society. I have also dealt with the effects that such rites can have on (a) The Autonomic Nervous System; (b) The Brain; (c) The Mental System; and (c) The Endocrine System; also the Chakras and their related glands, but more of (b) in a later Chapter, when all will be revealed.

Secret Societies - Beware!

In the past, so-termed 'secret societies' tended to be set up with the idea of preserving certain recondite knowledge, the nature of which was believed to be harmful to the uninitiated. There were secret Orders in the Egyptian, Babylonian and Roman Empires, as well as within minor kingdoms, and in their secrecy lay the key to their power. Details of secret organisations of the past - The Assassins, the Templars and the Secret Tribunals of Westphalia - have somehow found their way into later publications, although one is tempted to wonder at which point the fiction starts and the truth ends. However, I feel that there is one story which might serve as a cautionary tale for anyone who has it in mind to seek out, and endeavour to gain entry into a cult of this kind, no matter how many 'banners of light' it may choose to fly on its pinnacles.

Our story concerns one such organisation which was known as The Illuminati. Founded in Bavaria by one Adam Weishaupt in 1784, the Order was not basically Masonic although Weishaupt himself was a Mason, and introduced the Craft degrees into his system of Grades. Sadly, the suppression of this Cult in Austria was to have adverse effects on Masonry generally for some years to come.

Many strange stories have been told about Weishaupt and his plans for world domination which, to the rational thinker of today, might sound like the nineteen-sixties TV character - A.L.Wistey! (aka Peter Cook). Born in 'high places', Weishaupt was, at the age of 28, Professor of Law at Ingelstadt in Bavaria. Such a position having failed to satisfy his megalomania, however, he conceived the idea that man is born good and that all the wickedness and evils of the world stemmed from civilisation. Therefore, in order to restore mankind to its pristine goodness, civilisation as such needed to be destroyed. With the aid of two disciples, he set about overthrowing the thrones of the world with a view to gaining domination through anarchy and by assuming mystical control after the anarchy had been achieved. (Now where have I heard that one before - and more recently?)

However, with the aid of 'occult powers'(?) Weishaupt graded his pupils thus: Preliminary - Minerval, Minor Illuminatas, Major Illumini, Scottish Knight. The Mysteries - Priest, Regular Prince; The Greater Mysteries - Magus or Philosopher and Morn King. The Grade of 'Scottish Knight' was one in which he placed those who in reality were totally unsuitable for occult work, but who were useful in a political or financial sense. These 'Knights' were encouraged to think that they were the highest and that none were above them, thus were their egos flattered!

Weishaupt's *modus operandi* was to charge the Knights large sums of money for 'Initiation ceremonies' which would, albeit conveniently, result in their passing with flying colours and thus receiving the title of Grand Master, or some such appellation which carried great meaning in those times. However, his ruse was eventually discovered and he ended his days in prison. But doesn't this tale remind one of those so-termed 'Masters' in today's age, many of whom, I am given to understand, have parted with large sums of money in order to secure their metaphysical titles. Do things ever change?

CHAPTER 11

THE BASIC PRINCIPLES OF PSYCHIC SELF-DEFENCE

Is Psychic Protection Really Necessary?

In spite of what many may think, we are NOT automatically protected against intrusion by malevolent energies. Even so-termed 'good-living' people can be affected at some point in their lives. Sometimes, the more insensitive among us tend to fare better in that they are so totally orientated towards their basic instincts as to be unaware. There is obviously a great difference between the hallucinations of alcoholic over-indulgence (neural reaction to alcoholic poisoning) and a genuine psychic attack, and the same also applies to those who indulge in rich food and suffer horrific nightmares as a result. But does the food we eat affect our psychic senses? More than likely, it would seem. When I first aspired to step onto The Path, I was advised against eating red meat at any time, a rule which I have observed to this day.

I recall an instance which I mentioned in an earlier book on this subject, when an elderly couple present at a channelling session (we used to call it trance mediumship in those days) took umbrage when they noticed the Chairman placing a protection around the medium, and challenged him as to why such a precaution was necessary? 'To check the identity of the communicating entity, and ensure that it is of The Light', he replied. The couple in question seemed to take offence at this statement, declaring that they had 'been in this line of business for over 25 years and never encountered anything 'evil''. To which the able chairman replied, 'Well, Madam, you have obviously not disturbed it', the implication being that one cannot cast light about without exposing the nasties in the dark corners, who naturally take offence at the intrusion.

THE BASIC PRINCIPLES OF PSYCHIC SELF-DEFENCE

To be practical, how many of us would think of crossing a busy street without first checking the oncoming traffic, or any other obstacle that may bestride our path. Few in their right mind would act so rashly, and yet otherwise sane and stable people will happily plunge their thinking mechanisms into unknown or uncharted areas of consciousness without observing the simplest precaution. This naturally gives rise to the question, 'What is there to be afraid of and why should we need to protect ourselves?' If our intentions are honest, and we have a sincere desire for all that is righteous and correct, will it not be a question of like attracting like? Would that the Universe was that simple to comprehend. Surely history alone bears witness to the fact that even at the level at which we exist here on Earth, kindness, love, generosity of spirit and similar admirable virtues do not always result in our being able to surround ourselves with those of like mind. In fact, more often than not the essentially 'good' person will become the selected target for those who pursue the life of violence, hatred and debauchery. So why should it be any different on 'the other side'? After all, those included in the latter category are unlikely to change simply because they have 'passed on', a fact to which any exorcist worthy of his or salt will certainly avow.

Genuine psychics are able to tap into the collective unconscious of their own species and, on rare occasions, the group consciousness of other life forms such as the Elemental Kingdoms, Eyani (Paschats), Ishnaans (Crystal People), Olan (Dolphin Beings), Na-as (Plant Entities) and, reaching further afield, the Lizard People from the Capella System in the constellation of Auriga.

Since like inevitably attracts like, however, with whom, what and from where any psychic effects his/her contacts will naturally be decided by his/her soul age (field band-width in metaphysical parlance). All souls (fields) carry a specific energy potential which may or may not accord with that of the Being with whom they are hoping to communicate. Should the energy-potential of such a Being be incompatible with that of the medium, the transmission is often 'relayed' down the line via less exalted souls whose field data-banks may not possess the terms appropriate to the real message. The result? A garbled and often totally incorrect version of the intended 'teaching', or instruction. Over the years I have collected more evidence to support this 'psychic flaw' than a single, and somewhat restricted, tome could accommodate.

In spite of all the chaos that sometimes dogs the world of psychism, however, this Universe (and the next one, and the next one, ad infinitum) is not a haphazard conglomeration of differing life-cycles. It follows an organized pattern which accords with natural laws that are re-echoed in science, psychology and everyday existence. The apparent cycle of birth and death (as it affects the material worlds) or constant change as applied to areas of experience which take them through the fuzzy, quantum worlds of 'non-locality', is consistent in all dimensions as each Universe effects its inhalations and exhalations. When the life forces flow with the forward directional impulses of Cosmic Law the results are harmonious, but when any mind or intelligence seeks out the opposing path of Chaos, something or somebody will suffer as a result.

The Nature of Evil

There are many people who do not accept the existence of evil either as a force or a series of entities, believing it to be simply a facet of negative thinking which can be easily counteracted by either ignoring its existence or thinking pleasant and loving thoughts. This is all very cosy if the other fellow follows the same line of logic and avoids stirring up the mud but, sadly, the planet upon which we dwell is far from a haven of brotherly love, and the power generated by centuries of war, violence and hatred alone produces sufficient unstable energy to cause untold suffering at far more levels than the purely material!

Cosmic energy itself is a totally impersonal force, which only serves to reflect the image cast upon it by those experiencing within its limitless boundaries. So it is in everyday life: we may use a fire to warm ourselves, heat our water, make ourselves more comfortable in chillier climes; or we can torch our neighbour's abode, or manufacture bombs that will ignite the flames of suffering for all creatures extant on our poor, long-suffering planet.

What is generally termed 'evil' is energy operating against the forward directional impulses of Cosmic Law or to quote my Paschat friend, who makes a better job of explaining it than I could hope to do:

THE BASIC PRINCIPLES OF PSYCHIC SELF-DEFENCE

'Evil is misplaced or misdirected energy that is out of its correct time sequence. But there are many forms of evil, and to simplify it in this way might well give you the idea that we are denying its existence. Far from it. Of course it exists, but only as relative to time. A cannibalistic primitive would appear barbarous in the light of the accepted codes of behaviour in your present day world, whereas a few thousand years hence your present generation will be seen as bloodthirsty, warring savages by the standard of ethics then attained to.

Anything that transgresses Cosmic Law, meaning that which does not flow with its impulses, could be labelled 'evil'. Those who choose to run counter to the cosmic flow automatically set in motion a series of opposing energies that assume form as they gather momentum, eventually becoming a collective identity which feeds greedily on all that is around it. This misplaced force-field can be utilized by intelligences that have chosen to abandon temporarily the ways of Light and Love. Thus what are broadly referred to as 'evil forces' assume personalities according to the religious or philosophical inclinations prevalent in the age in which they first manifested.

Were your society correctly orientated time-wise much of what is generally termed 'evil' in your world would not exist. Of course there will always be those tensions that are part and parcel of the experience offered in each time-zone which usually result from the group or collective thinking of the race or planet in question.

This concept has given rise to what you call dualism, or the idea that the forces of good and the forces of evil are in constant counterbalance. In one sense this is a fair assessment, for each time-zone does present relative tensions against which those functioning within that circuit can push and thrust. It is only when the accumulated potential of that tension-mode becomes out of hand or out of balance that the resulting force-field lends itself for utilization by energies incompatible with Cosmic Law. The troubles then commence, as with your Earth.

Certain errant energies can only operate within a given wave-band: poltergeist phenomena, for example, which results from an involuntary release of undisciplined psychokinetic energy.

Misplaced or misdirected energy is by its very nature destructive, unless it is negated by its opposing force or anti-zone. There is an anti-zone for everything, and we Paschats (Eyani) and our Crystal Friends (Ishnaans) learned to negotiate incompatible energy fields, initially with sensitive deflective instruments and later by the use of pure mind power. The latter method entails mentally projecting the wayward energies into their appropriate anti-zone, or in the case of genuinely lost essence-fragments, returning the psyche in question to where it really belongs. Some of your occultists have already discovered how to inhibit phenomena in a similar manner and help rehabilitate lost fragments, these being the first stages in the technique'.

The Lion People, pp. 61-63, Thoth Publications, 1991.

Psychic Attacks

Over the years I have frequently been approached by people claiming to have experienced a 'psychic attack', and requesting that I promptly banish the cause of the problem. In ninety-nine per cent of such cases, there has been no external interference whatsoever, the 'fear' syndrome having been induced by a variety of psychological causes from anxiety to frustration. But on those rare occasions when I have been able to detect interference from an alien energy, the person in question is not all that innocent, having usually done something to attract it. The average person going about their daily business is unlikely to become possessed, or taken over by some disembodied entity intent upon wrecking his/her life and sanity. In fact more often than not, the cause of many such manias is to be found in the neural mechanisms of the brain, which can easily become addled by excesses of alcohol or drugs. So, what such people really need is a psychiatrist, not an exorcist.

On the other hand, the recent, media-encouraged interest in the psychic arts having spawned the popularity of mediums and psychics generally, there are certainly more than a few who claim to possess such gifts who are in it purely for the money. Aside from fleecing the gullible (a fool and his money being easily parted, as the old saying goes), few, if any, such practitioners actually effect any psychic damage on their clients. However, I can vouch for the fact that there are such things as psychic attacks, having experienced them myself. But then I elected to tread the hard path of the occultist, and if one chooses to cross the proverbial moors on a dark night in the full knowledge that there is a bogeyman lurking around out there, then the test is obviously to face up to the spectre and, if necessary, despatch it to some frequency more congenial to its evolutionary status. There is, of course, always the chance that it might have the same fate in mind for you, and therein lies the Initiation. Fail, and you could be found the following morning suffering from the effects of exposure (if the 'enemy' happens to be an 'elemental'), or sorely in need of a psychiatrist and a spell in a psychiatric hospital. Advice - if you don't like the heat stay out of the kitchen. In other words, unless it is your Karma to tread the Path of Magic steer well away from anything even vaguely connected therewith.

But as the average psychic does not work at that particular level, there is little chance of those anxious for a good reading becoming caught up in the web of bad nightmares, ghoulies, ghosties and things that go bump in the night. When dealing with the subject of Exorcism in the following Chapter, I will render several examples of people who were genuinely under some form of psychic attack, as against those whose problems were purely psychological or cerebral.

The Effect of Drugs and Other Artificial Stimuli

Psychic, occult or meditative work should never be undertaken while under the influence of any form of artificial stimulus. Contrary to what some addicts might say, drug induced 'trips' simply serve to cause certain areas of the brain to present a series of sensations or experiences which tend to bend the consciousness 'sideways'. In other words, the experimenter merely accesses that which is already within his/her neural databanks (software). Brilliant colours, lovely landscapes, visions of Buddha, Christ, angels, spacemen, all are familiar reference points in the history of human consciousness. If something is experienced which the neural software lacks the terms of reference to express, some abstract symbol may surface, but what many trippers do not seem to realise is that with a little self-discipline and the correct training, they may sample - at no cost - more wonders of the Universe than drugs could ever produce, while also effecting a positive control over their journeys - no more bad trips!

Time Symbols

The above is the name I have coined to describe broadly such divinatory aids as the Runes, I Ching, Tarot, or my own Cartouche, to name but a few. The great psychiatrist Carl Jung attested to the effect of symbology on the human psyche. When viewing an emblematic picture such as those depicted on Tarot Cards, or my Olympus deck, the symbology itself can have a subliminal effect on the brain, causing it to relate to the imagery at a level beyond the boundaries of time as we know it. Meaningful symbols can also cause a stirring of inner knowledge within the viewer to the extent that they, as much as the reader, become aware of the true nature of what is being said, or surreptitiously suggested. Symbols in themselves can effect a good protection as long as the user has absolute faith in them. A Pantheist, for example, might feel safe wearing or using symbols relating to Pan or Gaia, such as trees, birds, plants, or the Elemental Four. Likewise the Qabalist with the Sephiroth of the Tree of Life; a Catholic - with his/her Crucifix or Rosary and so forth. I myself wear a golden miniature of the Goddess Sekhmet on a chain around my neck, which I only remove on certain occasions, when I secret it in some other place on my person. As well as acknowledging the deity in question both in her Egyptian Role, and as the Atlantean deity Khiet-Sin, Leonine Goddess of Protection and Retribution, I am also reminded of my days as a Paschat, and the constant presence of the feline spirits of those to whom I was very close in those far distant times. I have, however, covered this angle of the subject in much more detail in my book *Practical Techniques of Psychic Self-Defence* which, or so I am given to understand, might well be reprinted at some point in the not-too-distant future.

As for safety when channelling, I recall with horror how a medium I once met in the past told me of how she had been sitting in a session where another was, supposedly 'taking' the group, when a terrible entity took over the medium, who threw herself upon the floor uttering curses, while spitting at her horrified audience and frothing at the mouth. In the school of occult discipline in which I trained, NO ENTITY OF THIS NATURE WOULD HAVE BEEN ALLOWED IN THE ROOM, LET ALONE PERMITTED TO ACTUALLY TAKE OVER A MEDIUM UNDER MY CARE AND PROTECTION! But then, as a wily psychologist friend of mine remarked when I related the incident to him, 'Well, it was obviously something within herself that she had been suppressing,

So, as with the old 'primal scream' stuff, it probably gave her the opportunity to get it all out of her system.' Interestingly enough, I did hear subsequently that said lady had given up all psychic work and enlisted as an aid worker, having exorcised her own demons, no doubt - but then experience over the years has tended to incline me towards cynicism..

Until recently, psychic self-defence was two-dimensional in that it dealt only with the hominid soul's eternal conflict which centred around good and evil as defined by the religious beliefs extant in the present, and earlier cultures. Now all that has changed. Cosmology and neuroscience have opened up human consciousness to the concept of multidimensional timelessness. No longer are the visions of our beliefs the demons of Dante's Hell, or even the mental imbalances delineated by Freud and Jung. From henceforth the human psyche is destined to be exposed to new visions of both chaos and order which will, in turn, constitute the 'bogeymen' of the forthcoming millennia.

My closing advice with regard to psychic self-defence is therefore - if you aspire to be a psychic worker then learn your trade properly, as we all have to, through the avenues of good training on the one hand and careful and discriminatory practical experience on the other. Walk forward slowly and with vigilance, always remembering that like attracts like. Should you at any time harbour thoughts of hatred, envy, malice, or violence, remember there will always be those energies about, be they incarnate or discarnate, which your 'state of mind' will automatically attract. Think positively, surround yourself with love and light, and bear in mind that humility augers better for spiritual progress than an overdeveloped ego.

For those who have no psychic ambitions as such, but are a wee bit unhappy about dark places and nightmares, remember that darkness is only the absence of light, while nightmares can be simply a tool for the unconscious to rid itself of those hidden fears and dreads that are kept well in control during the hours of consciousness.

A final suggestion - animals make wonderful protectors against the so-termed 'forces of darkness', particularly cats, who are more adept at warding off evil than many people who fancy themselves to be greater, wiser and more spiritually advanced than they really are. Sometimes it is the animal, not the human, who is the saint!

CHAPTER 12

OCCULT SELF-DEFENCE

Curses, and How to Remove Them

What exactly is a curse? It is a field of adverse energy which has been generated either by another consciousness, or emanations from the recipients themselves which have rebounded on them (bad karma, in general esoteric terminology), which can be dispersed by a stronger force-field (according to the Law of Equalities), and replaced by a more appropriate energy (the 'never leave a vacuum' principle).

Some years ago I was approached by an Indian gentleman, a Yogi of great repute, who could do anything he liked with his body, which skills he frequently demonstrated publicly. Among his own people he was worshipped as a Saint and yet, in spite of the eulogisation, he had harboured a dark secret which even he was unable to deal with.

He engaged me in conversation during the course of which he made it quite clear that he had sussed my 'spiritual origins'. For a man of his exceptional gifts he was humble in demeanour, and therefore reluctant to seek my help in a matter which was sorely troubling him. Eventually, and after much coaxing, he told his tale. It appeared that his great-grandfather had inadvertently given grave offence to a 'Holy Man from the North', who happened to be visiting that area at the time. The Holy Man, incensed at what he took to be a grave insult, laid a curse on the grandfather and his family, to the fourth generation, as a result of which several members had died of a 'mysterious affliction' for which, he assured me, there appeared to be no known medical treatment either within his own culture or modern Western medicine. After some hesitation he braved the question: could I remove this curse once and for ever, thus alleviating not only his own suffering, but that of his family?

Knowing instinctively that I could do something to help him I agreed to take on his case, and this is how I handled it: The first thing I did was to project back in time to before the curse was first placed, take a look at the scenario that proceeded it, and examine the intention behind the provocation that sparked off the whole episode. In carrying out this exercise I discovered to my horror that there had been no conscious intention to offend the Holy Man, the whole episode resulting from a misunderstanding on both sides. My next move was to make contact with the spirit of the Holy Man and show him how and where the misunderstanding occurred. He was immediately filled with remorse and cancelled his curse forthwith, while also assuring me that he would effectively recompense those who had suffered unnecessarily.

Two of the sufferers, who had reincarnated in more recent times, were able to feel the desired affect almost immediately. The lady, who had been suffering from an illness, made a miraculous recovery, while the man inherited a considerable fortune from a benefactor to whom he had rendered some assistance in previous years. As for my friendly Yogi, he declared himself a 'new man' and vowed that henceforth, instead of using his powers for public demonstration, he would set his sights on a more spiritually rewarding path. Although he never contacted me again, I heard later that he had founded an ashram, which served to expand not only his own spirituality, but also that of the pupils whom he had chosen to 'serve'.

So, how did I do this? Simple: by the transference of energies from one part of time to another, which is something that any occultist over a certain rank should be able to achieve. However, as I cannot claim such an exalted status I am obliged to confess that such exercises come naturally to a Time Deva. Now that is just one way of dealing with a curse. Of course there are others.

Many curses have been incurred as a result of resentment against those who have meted terrible suffering and afflictions on the curser. In such cases one is often obliged to soften the blows on both sides before the karma incurred is cleared. A classic example of this is the famous curse made by Jacques de Molay, the last Grand Master of The Order of Knights Templars. De Molay was burned to death after being brutally tortured under the instructions of Philippe IV of France, who was aided and abetted by Pope Clement V, both men having been hell-bent on the complete destruction of the Knightly Order. Legend has it that with his last breath, de Molay challenged his persecutors with the statement that if he had been wrongly accused they would both die painfully shortly after, which is exactly what happened!

The Mechanics of Exorcism

I have used the 'time transference' technique many times when undertaking exorcisms, and here is one case in question which was among many featured recently in my autobiography.

The action took place on a large estate in the north, where part of the grounds were let out as stables. The lady in charge thereof used to take groups of people for long rides which all went very well until they reached a given point in the route, when the horses would show signs of distress resulting in several topples. Anxious to find out what was 'spooking' this particular spot, the lady sought help from Gillian (who always worked with me when she was able) and yours truly.

My first course of action was to project back through time to the period at which the haunting commenced, and there, sure enough, lay the root of the problem. I found myself in the Border Wars period. A small posse of soldiers was seated around as though waiting for something or someone. I asked them why they were waiting there. The corporal answered me: Our Captain has gone on ahead to recce, and our orders are to wait here until he gives us the all-clear. But he hasn't come back, and we dare not disobey an order. My next move was to make contact, through Time, with the Captain. This actually proved quite easy, as his spirit had already been trying hard to let me know that he himself had been killed, and his small group ambushed and slaughtered to a man. Using a particular type of 'time-linking' energy, and with Gillian's help, I managed to get the two factions together. Upon seeing their officer the men were delighted, and naturally asked how the war was going. 'It's all over now, men. We have won. You may return to your homes in peace'. Whereupon they immediately vanished and the hauntings ceased forthwith, thus allowing the horses to pass peacefully on their daily ride.

All exorcisms are not that easy, however, and one can come up against some pretty nasty forces, in which case the first thing one does is to take measures to inhibit the manifestation of phenomena. Since phenomena of any kind can only manifest within a given waveband on the electromagnetic scale, or 'time-frequency' if one is dealing with the energy of Time, one commences by 'upping' both frequencies in the area concerned, to a point at which these cannot be tolerated by the offending entity, and proceeds from there, by first issuing the Law of Challenge. But how is this frequency-changing done? I'm afraid that is something I cannot fully explain. All I know is that I cannot remember a time when I did not know how to do it. I certainly never learned it from anyone, Master or otherwise. I think we used to do it in the Old Country - but then I seem to recall some of the priests employing a kind of sonic gadget to achieve the same effect. I and my kind have always possessed this 'gift' if you can call it such, which possibly has something to do with the natural energies emitted by my 'field'. But the fact that these same energies can sometimes act as an irritant to the hominid field has resulted in my life being anything but easy.

Leaving devic energies aside, electromagnetism could well play a role in the exorcisms of the future. I recall watching a play on TV in the early seventies which was entitled 'The Stone Tapes' by author Nigel Kneale. The story featured a haunted mill which defied all the usual efforts of exorcism. A camera crew who had been monitoring these phenomena then had the bright idea of altering the electrical frequency in the area concerned, and brought in the necessary equipment to effect this change. It worked perfectly, and there was never a sign nor sound of a haunting to be heard there again. However, I can't help wondering what would have happened had the story represented a real situation and not simply a fictional tale? Working on the premise that nature inevitably hates a vacuum, something else would probably have been standing ready in the wings. Was it not Jesus who said words to the effect that if the door is not closed, shall not seven more enter?

Banishing Rites might be all well and good (and spectacular to observe, no doubt), but is it not quicker to effect the same result either my way, or by the use of a simple electro-magnetic emission? However, in the latter case one would probably need an occultist around somewhere in the background to help the lost soul, while also ensuring that the newly vacated 'space' was filled with an energy conducive to the well-being of the next inhabitants or users! For the latter purpose I always invoke archetypal energies appropriate to the residents. In the case of a mother and baby this would be one of the 'maternal' rays from whichever tradition I felt to be appropriate: Isis, Demeter, Kwan Yin, any aspects of the Earth Mother, or the Virgin Mary in the Christian convention. For a student it would be Thoth, Hermes, or any of the deities of learning; for the craftsperson: Ptah, Hephaestus, Wayland, and so forth.

The question which naturally arises is, of course, what to do with the entity one has dislodged. The one thing one must NOT do is to leave it wandering about in limbo. Therefore, the next task is to assess from the band-width of its field (soul age) where it really belongs, and aid it in its return thereto. Sometimes, particularly in cases of benign entities who have simply become lost in transit, so to speak, one needs to comfort and reassure that soul, and guide it gently towards a mystical scenario in which one knows it will feel comfortable and 'at home'. That is the enjoyable side of the procedure. It is amazing how many times one is called in to deal with the exorcism of a spirit who is totally unaware that it has actually departed from its physical body. The kindest way to deal with such cases is to seek out someone that person has loved, and whom he/she acknowledges to be 'dead', and put the two together. It works every time!

One question I am often asked is why some religious exorcisms fail to work, bearing in mind that 'exorcist' is actually one of the stages a Catholic priest passes through on his road to ordination (just in case all that has changed, I can assert that it was certainly so according to the Catechism I was obliged to learn by heart!). However, when it comes to the nitty gritty of exorcism, it would seem that the ability to pass this or that exam, or attain to some ecclesiastical position, is no guarantee of one's power as an exorcist, as the following true story will show.

My story-teller in this case was an aged Jesuit, and the tale goes thus: During a period when he was attached to a small mission in the outbacks of India, a distraught father approached him (accompanied by some twenty or more relatives) to seek his help in disposing of a demon which had attached itself to his teenage daughter. Armed with his bell, book and candle, our worthy Jesuit set forth to carry out the required exorcism, but hardly had he set up his pieces for the necessary ritual when the demon in question addressed him thus through the girl: 'You are wasting your time. Go ahead and play your little games if you wish, but you do not have the power to dislodge me.' However, the priest was not put off by his initial failure, as he had been taught that it sometimes took the power of more than one priest to send Old Nick on his way. He therefore sought the help of two more priests from neighbouring missions and the three of them together went about the required procedures. But before the first line of the initial invocation had passed their lips, the demon once again pre-empted them, speaking through the girl: 'Oh, dear, I see we have more company here today. Very amusing, I am sure. But please, gentlemen, do not waste your time, as I have no intention of moving out, no matter how hard you pray to your God.'

Becoming somewhat perplexed (and more than a little frustrated) by then, our Jesuit approached his Bishop, a wily old man who, being obviously better versed in the ways of such phenomena than his juniors, promptly declined to have anything to do with it. So, for the time being, the poor young girl was left with her demon, much to the frustration of the family. Attendance at the Jesuit mission dropped off, the locals having lost faith in the ability of its God to sort out their problem.

However, it came to pass that a certain Holy Man, accompanied by his chela (student/disciple), happened that way, whereupon the distraught father and his family immediately turned to the newcomer for help with his daughter's malady. Surrounded this time by a very large crowd, the guru bent down and took a few pinches of earth, to which he added his own spittle. As he was about to reach out to anoint the forehead of the girl, the demon spoke out with alacrity, 'All right, all right, I know that you are more powerful than I, so I am therefore obliged to leave this host forthwith. But I must say I've had a good time while it lasted!' Whereupon the girl collapsed in a heap, and, when she came round, all traces of the intruder were gone forever.

The grateful villagers lost no time in presenting themselves at the Jesuit Mission, eager to render full details of the miraculous event, while also demanding to know why all the power of the Church could not dislodge the entity, whereas the Holy Man was able to do so without a struggle. Needless to say, our Jesuit and his friends, being somewhat narked, decided to seek the guru with the idea of prizing out his secret. When the worthy cleric finally caught up with him, his approach was forthright: 'How is it that the power of the Holy Church of Rome, acting in the name of its Founder, Jesus Christ Himself, was insufficient to dislodge the Devil from that girl, and yet you, a lone mortal lacking the support of a Church or established faith, were able to put it to flight?' A broad smile spread across the old guru's weather-beaten face as his eyes met those of his querent. 'Ah, my son, it is like this: about God you think you are knowing much, but about the Devil you are knowing nothing!', whereupon his roughened, brown feet once again trod the soil of his native land, and his lilting laugh haunted the Jesuit for many a year to come. As we used to say in the Theatre, 'What an act to follow!'

Sadly, all religions do not see fit to treat the possessed in such a kind manner. I am reminded of a case in the national press a year or so ago when a woman believed to have been 'possessed' by some demoniacal forces, was 'shaken to death', by those of her family intent upon ridding her of the supposed demon. If I recall the case correctly the poor soul was, in fact, suffering from a severe mental illness, there being no 'devils' there to exorcise in the first place. If one looks back to the past, one cannot help wondering how many poor, mentally ill souls were tortured, or burned at the Stake because their symptoms were mistaken for those of 'possession'. Freud, Jung, and Co. - thank you for putting at least a few things into their correct perspective. The fine line between so-called 'possession' and mental illness, caused by either psychological or neural malfunction, is something which I shall be dealing with in an ensuing Chapter.

Earlier in the book I mentioned the need for a cancer entity to be 'exorcised' before a full recovery from that dreaded disease can take place, experience also having taught me that these cosmic limpets can be moved by exposure to a frequency which they cannot tolerate. The exorcism of a cancerous entity is an extremely dangerous procedure for even the most experienced exorcist to handle, so, if you are not sure, don't risk it! The unwelcome 'field', once dislodged from its 'host', will make for the nearest human with either an open, or loosely sealed aura. If you, the exorcist (or healer, as the case may be), do not possess the power or knowledge to return the offending entity to its rightful sphere of evolution, then I beg you to leave well alone. As I explained in Chapter 5, the old system Gillian and I used involved the 'coverer and caller' technique, which I abandoned after Gillian's passing. Since then I have always worked alone, although I have recently retired, my physical shell having taken just about enough of the trials and tribulations of the magical Path. My only contribution to the field of metaphysical knowledge now lies in my writing. It is my belief, however, that some individuals are immune to the cancer entity energy, simply because the frequency of their 'fields' inhibits its entrance into their auras in the first place. But that is something best left until such times as one is absolutely sure of either one's natural immunity, or one's skills in the time-movement of alien fields.

N.B. For those interested in the above, my autobiography features a whole chapter on my years as an exorcist, with full details of a number of the very difficult and diverse cases with which I dealt, earlier with Gillian, but latterly on my own.

Beware the Power Seekers

One of the reasons why I would never again work with a group or Lodge of any kind is, as experience has taught me, the constant jostling for power which inevitably seems to taint such organisations. I seem to recall being obliged to attend Committee meetings when I was President of The Atlanteans, although raising any issue that was not on the official agenda inevitably proved a waste of time since I was more than aware that a small segment of the group had probably got together beforehand and decided which way the votes would go. It therefore paid to pretend to nod off, and simply say 'yes, whatever you say', in order to keep the peace. There was one occasion when I did I adopt an opposing stance - with disastrous results, the details of which are best forgotten.

I have since conversed with many people who have either belonged to Lodges or metaphysical organisations of some sort or another and heard the same, sad tale. It really does pay to remember that many hominids have not as yet individuated from the Group

Collective, so it comes naturally to them to band together against anything they view as being 'the opposition'. Of course this tendency can also be read in the psychological sense, although it would seem that whether people are practising magic, or running committees, the 'conspiracy' mode is sure to rear its unwelcome head (or 'heads'?) at some point during future proceedings.

On the other side of the coin, however, it would seem that there are many who have a psychological need to work in groups with others. Well, if that is right for them, then so be it, and who am I to suggest otherwise. After all, I am only a temporary visitor to this planet!

The Dangers of Mixing Systems

As any metaphysical student worth his or her salt is well aware, each magical system exhibits its own, unique frequency, or specific type of energy, and, contrary to what some students of the magical arts would have it, incompatibilities between the various energies DO exist. Those among us who have effected an in-depth study of these phenomena are well aware of the inconsistencies involved, and I myself have included a list of 'Rays and Anti-Rays' in my book *Cosmic Connections* (Thoth Publications).

One of the tasks which I am frequently called upon to perform is cleaning up the psychological mess caused by those who will persist in putting on 'ritual performances' which include bits and pieces of several traditions, and inviting the public in to witness the entertainment. The mixing of incompatible Rays inevitably results in chaos, and those members of the public who have not been schooled in psychic or occult self-defence are usually the ones to suffer. The perpetrators of such outrages are guilty of acting in a totally irresponsible and dangerous way; but try to tell them that and one is greeted with such rejoinders as, 'Well, everybody seemed to be having a good time', or 'They absolutely loved the costumes.' But what about the next day, and the day after that? Not such good times for many, I fear. I have even heard of young girls of twelve and thirteen being 'initiated' into the priesthood of this or that ancient belief, without their being aware of the energies they are likely to be confronted with as a result, and the effect these energies are likely to have on both their general health, and their burgeoning hormonal reactions. It is little wonder that in one case which came to my notice, the youngster suffered considerable physical harm shortly after.

Is this just a symptom of the undisciplined age in which we live, or is it due to pure ignorance on the part of the perpetrators? I realise only too well that it is common practice these days for someone to read a couple of books, take a trip to Egypt, and return claiming to be an 'expert' who has the knowledge to actually write an instruction manual of Egyptian Magic! But then I have also seen books about the Deva Kingdoms (obviously not written by a Deva, or they would not contain such a veritable load of inaccuracies). But then, as a kindly, and occultly knowledgeable friend recently said to me, 'Horses for Courses', and even the ponies like to imagine they are running at Ascot at sometime in their lives! Sorry folks if I have come down too hard on you, but I do wish you would let the devas speak for themselves. Enough said.

The Ethics of Magic - Is Intention the Deciding Factor?

There is little doubt that the intention behind a Rite, or magical Working of any sort, with or without the attendance of ritual, does carry considerable weight, particularly in the karmic sense. It is therefore dangerous to undertake a Rite or Working for anyone who asks for help in the knowledge that any assistance you may give is likely to cause harm or suffering to another. Help can, of course, be given when ethics are involved, but the occultist should always avoid directing his/her energy at another person in an adverse way, even though this may be executed on behalf of a dear friend or loved one.

The best way to tackle such a problem would be to put the whole issue on The Scales of Maat, a simple Egyptian magical rite which involves visualising Maat's Scales and placing Her Feather of Truth on the Right hand Scale and the request of the querent on the other, and then energising the entire piece and slowly projecting it into the Higher Frequencies until it reaches a point when either a hand appears to take it, or it simply dissolves into a cloud of brilliant colour and light. In this way, one is placing the request in the hands of more exalted powers who, having a broader and clearer view than we have here on Earth, will channel the energy into an appropriate form of expression that will help the person in need, while also avoiding causing harm to others in the process.

It would be correct to say that in White Magic, intention is most important. Like inevitably attracts like, and if one persists in manipulating magical energies for selfish or perverse purposes, the one thing one can be sure of is that the 'bill' will appear through one's proverbial 'letterbox' sooner, if not later. Now that bill could involve anything from financial loss to ill health, so is it not better to stay on the straight and narrow in the first place? As I mentioned earlier the late Dion Fortune often referred to what she termed the 'Occult Police'. Believe you me, these do exist, and at all levels, so don't become complacent because you feel that their 'enquiries' may appear to be taking a long time: Remember, the 'Inner Planes' (as orthodoxy prefers to label them), are policed by Time Devas, and, I speak from first hand experience here, we know exactly when to push that proverbial summons through your mental letterbox!

CHAPTER 13

THE PSYCHOLOGY OF PSYCHISM AND MAGIC

The Eight Psychological Types

Psychology has spawned many offshoots since the days of Freud and Jung, Behaviourism, and the Transpersonal Schools being but two examples. My starting point should not, therefore, be taken as an indication as to my personal preferences.

Years of study and research have resulted in the more orthodox schools of psychology and psychiatry drawing up a broad set of classifications under the heading 'Psychological Types', experience having shown them that we all manifest behavioural symptoms of either one of these in particular or, in some cases, combinations thereof. As a serious student of psychology I have often been intrigued by the accuracy of these assessments, particularly in the world of magic and psychism, where aberrations tend to be thrown into stark contrast, thus enabling the observer to spot the problems quite easily. It is also interesting to observe which of these 'types' are best suited to either psychism (the receptive mode), or occultism (the directive mode). Perhaps, after perusing the following, you, the reader, may be able to identify yourself.

THE HYSTERICAL PERSONALITY

Contrary to popular belief this occurs in both males and females. Such people have an immature quality about them and a low tolerance threshold, which inclines them to sudden swings of mood and irrational outbursts. Much to the consternation and perplexity of those around them, they soon recover from these tantrums and proceed to act as though nothing untoward has occurred. In spite of being difficult and childlike they are never dull and often give a great deal of themselves to their friends and those they love.

THE OBSESSIONAL PERSONALITY

Obsessive types are conscientious, tidy, critical, punctual, pedantic and repetitive. They do not like change of any kind or alterations in their routines and they are reluctant to show their emotions. As they have difficulty in adapting to new ideas or concepts, they are best-suited to avenues of expression which are of a regular nature.

THE SCHIZOID PERSONALITY

This personality type lacks emotional warmth and friendliness, preferring his or her own company. Such people are not interested in others and are therefore unsociable, preferring to be left alone to do their own thing. They can make good careers for themselves, however, and frequently do well in research science and computer studies.

THE PARANOID PERSONALITY

Paranoiacs are touchy, oversensitive, and incapable of accepting criticism. Included in this group are those who feel that the whole world is out of step with them. Such people are difficult and almost impossible to work with, but under suitable social conditions they are capable of rising in the world through their own efforts, and may often be seen leading new groups or sects - Adolf Hitler being an example.

THE DEPRESSIVE PERSONALITY

I think we have all met those pessimists who turn every statement into a negative. If one tells them, for example, that one has a bad knee, they will inform one that both of their knees are bad - also their shoulder, stomach, and a few other parts of their anatomy. Likewise if one makes the mistake of mentioning to them that one is broke, or having emotional problems, one's woes are inevitably 'topped'. A sense of inadequacy is, of course, the problem here.

THE CYCLOTHYMIC PERSONALITY

These people react to life's situations with emotional excess, fluctuating between joy and despair, depression and elation, pessimism and euphoria. They are seldom, however, on a regular even keel. Like the depressive personality, they are plunged into deepest gloom by loss or failure, although their reaction to success is one of wild joy and abandonment. It is interesting to note that recent research into cases of manic depression as related to genius (the two frequently go together and are generally included under the cyclothymic heading) can be traced to a certain gene. In other words, the gift of genius and the personality discomforts that would appear to accompany it are, in many cases, inherited!

THE ANXIOUS PERSONALITY

People of this personality type are inevitably apprehensive, believing that disaster is lurking around every corner. If all is going well, they will search for something to worry about, and if there is nothing on the immediate horizon, then they will create it, or see its possibility in the future. Strangely enough, when faced with real difficulties, the anxious personality is often competent and decisive, but it is when he or she feels him or herself to be stagnating that the problems start.

THE NARCISSISTIC PERSONALITY

Here we have a person who is unable to separate his own feelings and needs from the people he encounters. All must reflect himself and his own needs and wants. Narcissistic people are prone to Mirror Complexes, in that they see their faults or idiosyncrasies in others rather than themselves. Such people love the limelight, and are able to achieve much in worldly status as long as their preoccupation with the self is well catered for. Hence they are to be found among celebrities of the entertainment and political worlds, or any sphere of life which caters for the ego-conscious.[1]

Very few people represent any one of these groups in toto: most of us are somewhat of a mixture. None the less, these groupings may help us recognise more obvious personality traits that could aid the assessment of our strengths and weaknesses.

However, for those who may feel the above categories to be too psychopathologically orientated, there is an alternative Jungian Model which incorporates the four Elemental personality aspects, while also according with the twelve astrological archetypes:

```
Fire   - the Intuitive function
Air    - the Thinking function
Water  - the Feeling function
Earth  - the Sensate function [2]
```

The Introvert/Extrovert complex might also be of interest to the reader, certain schools of mysticism/psychism tending to attract one or other of the two.

The Introvert/Extrovert Complex - Psychological Identifications

INTROVERTED

Passive	Quiet
Careful	Unsociable
Thoughtful	Reserved
Peaceful	Pessimistic
Controlled	Sober
Reliable	Rigid
Even-tempered	Anxious
Calm	Moody

STABLE   **UNSTABLE**

Leadership	Touchy
Carefree	Restless
Lively	Aggressive
Easygoing	Excitable
Responsive	Changeable
Talkative	Impulsive
Outgoing	Optimistic
Sociable	Active

EXTROVERTED

Even a cursory glance at the above might help the would-be psychic or occultist to identify which side of the polarity they feel best suited to, if any. For example, an Hysterical type should avoid the whole psychic-cum-magic scenario at all costs, and ditto the Paranoid, Depressive, Cyclothymic and Narcissistic. Obsessional personalities would probably fare well in some of the more austere magical systems such as the Norse or Qabalistic, and likewise the Schizoid, but the best type to have around in any occult emergency is obviously the Anxious Personality. Narcissistics can make good media clairvoyants, their best 'work' obviously manifesting when they are in the public eye, but I wouldn't care to have a reading with a Depressive type - I might come away with the woes of the world on my shoulder! I have known some Cyclothymiacs who are brilliant psychics on occasions, but although they can display moments of psychic genius, the reliability of their performance will depend very much on their mood of the moment.

Although as far as the Introvert/Extrovert system is concerned, stability is not necessarily an indication of occult or psychic prowess. I would prefer to put my faith in a stable Introvert. But then I am not over-impressed by easy-going, social types.

In his book *Explaining the Unexplained*, Professor Hans J. Eysenck, commenting on why extroverts are better ESP subjects, tells us:

> It is fairly well established that extroverts have lower levels of cortical arousal (activity in the cortex of the brain) than introverts. This may, in part, be because extroverts are better at suppressing the activity of nerve cells in the medulla (the base of the brain) which relay incoming sensory signals to the cortex.[3]

For those interested in the parapsychological approach, the above mentioned book is a veritable mine of both information and evidence.

Psychology also offers us another series of terms which call for interpretation. For example, Freud defined the personality as having three vital strands: the id, the ego and the super ego, the former being totally unconscious and the latter two a mixture of conscious and unconscious. The 'id', sometimes referred to as the animal energy, is concerned with instinctive impulses and demands for immediate gratification of primitive needs and desires. As the boiling cauldron of the personality, it represents a strong force which often finds expression in fantasies. Being amoral, it has no sense of right and wrong; hence its association with man's darker nature. Desire, aggression and need are said to emanate from the id, and its power to affect our physical responses may be evidenced in the sexual effects of fantasising. On the other hand, religious fantasising has been known to produce stigmata, as I mentioned earlier in this book, so I do not feel that we can necessarily allocate all somatic responses to mental stimulus to the chthonic regions.

The ego was viewed by Freud as the conscious driving force that controls the id and prevents it from having its own way, the ego only allowing the id to fulfil those desires which are not to its detriment. Following Freud's death, a group of psychologists, led by his daughter Anna, broke away from his original concept, believing that the ego has its own store of energy which enables it to satisfy its personal, social and creative needs independent of, and without conflict with, the id. Today, however, the term ego is more generally used to denote the 'I', or unique expression of the individuality rather than the mind or the psyche. While Freudian psychology views the ego as a personal value system, the upper layer of the personality, or super-ego, is seen as an amalgam of belief systems based on external standards set by society, its main role being to suppress the unseemly desires of the id by forcing the ego to ignore all the id's basic urges. Its reward, should it succeed in its mission, is societal approval.

The popular use of the term 'psyche' can probably be attributed to the work of the late Carl Gustav Jung, who deviated from Freudian thinking in his belief in the collective unconscious. He called the whole personality the psyche and maintained that it has three levels: the ego, which is the conscious mind; the personal unconscious, in which is stored all our repressed fantasies, dreams and desires; and the collective unconscious, which is part of the primordial past and which each of us inherits. It is from the latter that we derive our image of archetypes, which prove so important in subconscious communication and therefore exert a profound effect on our state of balance or otherwise. Jung also conceived of the 'shadow' or darker side of the self, which needed to be faced up to and overcome.

Many three-fold references have appeared since the time of Jung and Freud, although there are an equal number which were acknowledged in metaphysical circles long before the advent of modern psychiatry; the natural/instinctive, rational/intellectual and creative/intuitive, for example, and the three-fold nature of the Triple Goddess - maiden/mother/crone - each of which represent different aspects (or spiritual growth stages) of the whole psyche or self. The term 'psyche' is also used among certain groups to describe either the superconscious, higher or transpersonal (all-knowing) self, or the soul/spirit (field), which is believed by many to be the spark or intelligence that gives life to the body and programmes the brain - to which I would add, once the individuation process has taken place and the person/persons in question are capable of programming their own brains. This brings me back full circle to the psychology versus mysticism debate, with all that this entails. As for the brain itself, new knowledge regarding its neural propensities and functioning are being discovered with such rapidity that yesterday's reference books (and this book, no doubt), are out of date almost before they leave the printers.

Special studies have also been effected between a person's physiology and their mental make-up. The late Dr. Charlotte Wolff, who was a student of the celebrated psychiatrist Ernst Kretschmer, wrote several books on this psycho-physical phenomenon, which seem to have been borne out in later studies. In other words, our appearances can certainly give us away - well - to the experienced eye, anyway!

Taking into account the different psychological types, each with its pluses and minuses, would it not be prudent for all those aspiring to either aspect of the mystical polarity (psychic or occultist), to effect a self-analysis in the light of the above, and ask themselves whether they are really psychologically suited to their chosen metaphysical roles? While there are inevitably times when Doubt wraps her sinuous shroud around us, if we are totally honest with ourselves and able to dispense with the sly nudges of self-delusion, inspiration from genuinely exalted sources will always come to our aid to light our Path ahead. Then we will know for sure.

Know Your Archetypes

It is now known that both psychological 'mismanagements', (phobias, etc., and faulty neural 'software') can easily be corrected by reprogramming, and although there are some practitioners who choose to think to the contrary, psychology and neuroscience are inextricably bound to the mystical arts. In fact, recent clinical and psychological studies in both these fields are serving to throw new light on what has hitherto been viewed as mumbo-jumbo. It is therefore advisable for the student to possess at least a modicum of knowledge of these twinned studies, be that either academic or natural, in order to effect a comprehension of what is going on in both the psyche and the brain during occult and psychic procedures. Learning to identify with one of the acknowledged metaphysical archetypes (see my Olympus and Cartouche Cards, etc.), or above mentioned psychological categories, will serve to highlight both one's strengths and weaknesses, and the specific areas in which both of these are likely manifest.

Those who seek to tread the metaphysical path, in either of its polarities (a) receptive or, (b) directive, would therefore be well advised to give some thought to (i) the psychology behind their interpretations and the effect these are likely to have on the life or lives of their querents and (ii), the direction and causes to which their energies are applied. Care should be taken to ensure that there are no 'leaks' which could produce painful side-effects of one kind or another somewhere along the line. It has come to my notice on many occasions how certain persons are invited to attend Rites without aforethought as to whether or not they are psychologically equipped to handle the energies that might possibly manifest during the proceedings.

In psychology an experimental result is only as good as the experimental process, and although the object of the exercise may be nominal, the same principle applies to the world of the paranormal. The procedure is to set up a protocol which provides knowledge, experience and quality assurance, and is programmed to deliver a uniform result - the sensitisation of the recipient.

Whenever there is a manifestation of preternatural energy at any level the inevitable catalyst is to be found 'somewhere in the wings', and this applies as much in metaphysics as in psychology.

Studies in schizophrenia have shown that some patients are affected by such things as phases of the Moon and other atmospheric phenomena, a fact to which any psychiatric nurse will avow. But then are we not dealing with one at least of the four acknowledged sources of energy on this planet - gravity, electromagnetism and the weak and strong nuclear forces, as I have mentioned in an earlier chapter? Time has now also entered the picture, although as yet there has been little attention paid to its possible influence on the human psyche. I refer again to James McDonald's description of the energy emitted by Time as, 'psychotronic - a kind of material radiation not of our technology and external to the human brain'. So, as this realisation slowly percolates throughout the scientific community, there are bound to be questions as to the effect it has on our cerebral mechanisms. We know, for example, that our movement through time (or time's movement through us?) actually ages the body so, as the saying goes - watch this space.

How much so-termed psychism is genuine and how much the product of schizophrenia and associated mental disorders is something the psychologists and psychiatrists are still trying to discover. Schizophrenia itself is divided into four sub-groups, called Hebefrenia, Catatonia, Paranoid and Simple, each manifesting its own particular symptoms some of which, sad to say, may be seen to resemble those displayed by psychics and mystics worldwide.

One of the areas of human experience much loved by psychologists is that of dreams, although the debate is still on when it comes to differentiating between a genuine astral encounter during sleep state and a neural/somatic experience caused by either psychological stress or food intake. This brings us back full circle to my statement in an earlier part of this book - that some aspects or fragments of our 'fields' exist simultaneously in parallel universes. The latter being the case, then should we not be able to effect changes at the earthly level by our actions and experiences undergone during sleep? As for nightmares and other garish nocturnal encounters - are these purely cerebral/psychological, or do we actually encounter negative/chaotic energies while surfing the Internet of Nod?

The trouble with all this cross-analysis is that one can so easily become caught up in the complexity versus reductionism debate, my answer to which is very simple - half a dozen of one and six of the other!

While on the subject of the psychology versus metaphysical disputation, much has recently been written concerning such Eastern beliefs as the Kundalini experience which, according to Indian tradition, is a type of energy, force or power (shakti) that is held to rest in a dormant, or potential state, in the human body. Its location is generally specified as being at the base of the spine, although, when 'awakened', it will proceed upwards along the spinal column to the crown of the head, triggering off various states of consciousness during its ascension. Upon reaching its goal - which some visualise as actually being above the head, it is believed to confer a state of ecstatic mysticism which is described as being 'indescribably blissful'. The energy contacted by this rising Kundalini is said to be the power that precedes, and also simultaneously invades the entire cosmos. For those interested there are several books available on the subject, but if asked for my personal opinion I am obliged to admit that I have never practised the type of meditation/yoga which is believed to be conducive to the Kundalini Experience, nor am I ever likely to, since I am able to move my consciousness (field) through this (and several other) universes at will. As for the ecstatic state, I, and several others I know and respect, are also able to partake of that state of 'bliss' by such simple actions as observing the beauty in a flower, cuddling a beloved animal, or enjoying the warmth and love of dear friends. Why do the mystics always insist that we must look to some fabled sphere for inspiration and/or spiritual 'highs' when all is present around us, had we but eyes to see it! As the old Hermetic Axiom goes: 'As above, so below!' Enough said on that score.

I was once asked whether the Earth had chakras, or their planetary equivalent. There are indeed certain 'points' on her surface which correspond to related 'qualities' as manifest through the human and other life-systems. I have actually lectured on this subject and met with almost unanimous agreement as to the location of these 'planetary energy centres'. But as this subject-matter forms part of another study in itself that would call for a book to do it justice, this seems an appropriate point at which to bow out of the psychology debate.

The Occult Side-Effects of Drugs and Other Artificial Stimulants

Although I have already commented on the above in the previous Chapter, it cannot be emphasised enough that all forms of drugs or medication which in any way affect the brain, consequently influence adversely the expression of those aforementioned 'gifts; and this applies to any person, no matter who he or she may be, or whatever mystical talents or exalted ranks he or she may claim to have attained to. Although the following instance applies more to the previous Chapter, it also highlights the need for an 'occult coverer' who could have corrected it in the first place. The story was told to me of one normally 'very good' medium who, after a few drinks, delivered a load of nonsense which, on the following day when he was sober, was angrily repudiated by his 'guide', who stated in no uncertain terms that the message given was most certainly not from him, but simply the result of 'the addled thinking of the medium's brain, his perspective having been altered by the booze'! .

On one occasion when I was lecturing at a large Metaphysical Conference, one of the other speakers, who had himself been a drug-user, assured his audience that although he did experience 'strange visions' when under the influence, none of these ever featured anything new, merely an albeit colourful rehash of what he already knew. He described these narcotic visions as 'looking neither up nor down, but sideways'. In other words, no matter what you imbibe with a view to entering a more pleasant mode of consciousness, once within that mode you can never exceed your neural programme extant at the time.

Personally, I have never had a problem with so-termed 'seeking'. But then that, perhaps, is one of the, albeit few, advantages of being a devic soul in an earth body - one always has access to the data-banks of one's own kind!

As a (hopefully?) useful ending to this chapter I have devised a questionnaire for both psychics and occultists, which may serve to jog their conscience, while also affording them some psychological (and ethical) guidelines to follow when dealing with their clients, or students as the case may be.

Questionnaires For (a) Psychics, (b) Occultists

PSYCHICS

1. When first meeting your client, are you able to recognise his/her psychological type, and structure your reading accordingly? For example, it is of no help to the paranoid client to be told that they have 'got it all wrong' or effected an erroneous judgment, for from that moment on they will naturally dismiss anything you say as rubbish.

2. When mentioning events likely to take place in the future, are you specific about dates? Because if you are, and that date passes without incident, the querent (especially if he/she is an anxious personality type) having built up his/her hope, could become worried or even traumatised as a result.

3. Are you careful to assess your client's social and educational background and couch your advice in terms familiar to this/her standard of perception? Psychological terminology may be appropriate when conversing with a University graduate or professional person, but a more 'homely' approach would be better suited to those less familiar with academic jargon. In simple terms - never talk either 'up' or 'down' to a client.

4. Do you try to avoid putting the 'fear of God' into your client, especially if he/she happens to be an hysterical or paranoid personality type? For example, should you perceive psychically a disaster which cannot be averted, employ a cursory warning only - thus avoiding any possible panic attacks which might result later.

5. Are you able to keep your own ego out of the picture? (A friend of mine consulted a well-known seer who spent the first twenty-minutes of the session relating details of her former psychic triumphs!)

6. Do you 'up' your fee if your client is observed to be wearing expensive jewellery and designer clothes?

OCCULTISTS

1. Do you encourage interested parties to effect their own choice of systems and, should that choice vary from that of your Group or Lodge are you able to let them go with your blessing and refrain from inferring that they have 'taken a wrong turning' simply because they have not elected to follow in your exact footsteps?

2. When accepting a neophyte into your Group or Lodge are you careful to ensure that he/she is not exposed too early in the proceedings to energies that could disturb his/her mental balance before the brain has had time to update its neural software?

3. Is your organisation money-orientated? Do you take on students purely on the grounds that they can afford to pay the fees you are asking (presumably for the esteemed value of your tuition!)? A person's bank balance should be no indication as to their suitability to the Magical Path (remember the Scottish Knights?) If they have a modicum of common sense they will suss you for what you are, anyway!

4. When faced with a Rite that misfires, causing one or more of those present to enter a state of hysteria, are you able to cope without your bell, book and candle, and treat the sufferer in the same way as a psychologist or doctor would do - with a smart slap round the face, which practice will have a better 'earthing' effect than all your Banishing Rites and invocations. Remember, everything to its own level, and hysteria is a medical condition.

5. Do you have the humility to acknowledge any errors of judgment on your part and set about correcting these? When faced with the Initiation Factor, are you so steeped in the occult practices of the past that you cannot adjust to a new energy influence. While taking care not to throw out the proverbial baby with the bath-water, are you capable of creating your own horizons, getting out of that ancient groove and embracing the worlds of psychology, the sciences, and cosmology in particular. After all, was that not the way of the great sages and occultists of the past?

6   Instead of settling for the accustomed 'high' that certain, familiar Rites can sometimes accord, try to remember that occultism encompasses the study of ALL universes and ALL therein. In other words, cosiness and familiarity may give you that feel-good factor, but it is the acquisition of true cosmic knowledge that should be the aim of the genuine occultist.

1   *The Psychology of Healing pp.39-42. Element Books, Shaftesbury, 1989.*
2   *Practical Solitary Magic p.115. Samuel Weiser Inc. York Beach, ME.,1996.*
3   *Explaining the Unexplained p.51. Weidenfeld & Nicolson, London, 1982.*

CHAPTER 14

THE BRAIN - A BIOLOGICAL COMPUTER

Who (Or What) Effects Our Neural Programming?

Back in the nineteen-fifties, in the days when the Caxton Hall in London was available for lectures, I stood on the platform there and stated categorically that the human brain was a computer, nothing more or less. It has taken science forty years to arrive at the same conclusion! I recall explaining to the audience that just as a computer needs to be programmed, so, also, do our brains, and that this neural input could be effected from a variety of sources such as social, ethnic and religious programming, soul-age (field band-width) and genetics, to name but a few. Catholic officials are often heard to say 'give us a child before he/she is seven and we will give you a Catholic for life'. So powerful is this early neural programming that people I have known who have abandoned that religion at some stage in their middle life, have inevitably returned to it in their mature years. The only people to escape from such traps are those who are able to discard all previous programmes and insert their own, chosen brand of neural software. In other words, those experiences which life accords us over the years can serve to create an individual program for each of us which we either unconsciously or consciously enter into our neural data-banks, and then proceed to act upon - ethically, morally, practically and spiritually, until such times as experience demands an adjustment of either addition or subtraction, or when our physical shells are finally returned to the elements via whose kind offices we have the use of physical bodies in the first place.

Here are a few snippets of interesting information concerning the brain that have come to light during the last few years:

Scientists claim that they have discovered the first proof that intelligence depends on our genes. This, they say, could be a vital clue in the development of intellect, compared to education and upbringing. (The old Nature/Nurture debate raises its hoary head yet once more!) The research team, led by Dr.Robert Plomin, a leading behavioural geneticist from the US working at the Institute of Psychiatry in London, and his colleague, Professor Jeffrey Gray, made their breakthrough by taking samples from 50 bright children whose exam scores were equivalent to an IQ of 160 or higher. The genetic markers were then compared to those of children who were of average intelligence. It is believed that the gene they isolated may be only one of around fifty genes which are responsible for determining how clever we are. The research, reported in the Journal of Psychological Science, is at present being checked by other scientists. Dr. John Kihlstrom, a psychologist at the University of California at Berkeley, added: 'It's the first time that a gene has been associated with some specific aspect of cognition and behaviour'. From recent research it would seem that men's brains deteriorate three times faster than those of women: in a recent study carried out at Pennsylvania University, Dr. Reuben Gur of the human behaviour laboratory, discovered that men's brain cells die off far more rapidly than women's. The parts of the brain which die off first are those responsible for reasoning. Dr. Gur believes this finding explains why old men are usually far grumpier than old women. He also suggests that his findings should lead to a reversal of present retirement ages, where women retire earlier than men. Scientists tell us that within five decades the last great mystery, consciousness, will be reduced to a comprehensible mechanical process, leaving science with something of an existential crisis. The size of one's brain is irrelevant - some mammals, notably dolphins, have larger brains than humans!

I have a file full of such pieces of information, much of which could probably merit adjustments in the light of new research.

So what do we really know about the human brain and is such knowledge relevant to the world of metaphysics? From the metaphysical standpoint, human consciousness can be classified into five aspects, or areas of experience, each of which are accommodated by appropriate neural software:

THE INSTINCTIVE	(Earth)
THE INTUITIVE	(Water)
THE RATIONAL	(Air)
THE INSPIRATIONAL	(Fire)
THE EXPANSIONAL	(Time)

The basic design of the brain, and its pre-programming facility, is readily observable in the process of one part of the brain taking over from another. This may be evidenced in the phenomena of phantom pain experienced following limb removals, while it is known medically that if, for example, a foot is removed, an area of the brain which is normally associated with another organ can compensate for that loss. Scientists tell us that we see with our brains and not with our eyes, the external organs being merely conveniences for the output and input of imagery.

In 1976, Princetown psychologist Julian Jaynes effected his contribution to the neural debate in a work entitled *The Origin of Consciousness In The Breakdown of the Bicameral Mind*, which dealt specifically with the different neural functions undertaken by each 'side' of the brain. As is now acknowledged, the right hemisphere deals with creativity, spatial perception, abstract thought and musical and visual appreciation, while the left hemisphere is concerned with logic, analytical abilities and day to-day factual matters. However, according to Jaynes, the left hemisphere was not active in early man, the watershed having occurred as recently as 1250 B.C. Jaynes' starting point is the relatively new science of split-brain physiology, which now has to be taken into consideration when analysing the neural abilities of those civilisations which we know existed prior to the date given by Jaynes.

In his book *The Runaway Brain*, Christopher Wills quotes the following observation effected by Julian Huxley in his *Evolution in Action* (1953):

> Granted that natural selection is the only effective agency for producing change in biological evolution, a high degree of mental activity could only come into being if it was of biological advantage to its possessors. This at one stroke overthrows all theories of materialism, for they deny the effective reality of mind, or reduce it to a mere fly on the material wing. (p.245)

The Neuro-Mechanisms of Religion

Prior to the commencement of this work, I read a review of a book entitled, *Mapping The Mind*, by Rita Carter, a medical writer, who was twice awarded the Medical Journalists' Association prize for outstanding contribution to medical journalism. I was sufficiently impressed by this work to effect an in-depth study of the information featured therein, with the intention of aligning it with the higher grades of esoteric knowledge. One of the first observations of metaphysical note was the 'biological basis of mental illness', which, the author tells us, is now demonstrable. Similarly, the neural mechanics which prompt such outbursts as rage, violence and misperception, while on the gentler side - kindness, humour, altruism, mother love and self-awareness can also be physically observed by neurologists. Carter refers to humanity's constant attempts to effect an alteration of consciousness through drugs, sensation-seeking and self-entrancement (channelling?), and how it may soon be possible to attain to higher levels of consciousness 'without any of the usual drawbacks'. It would seem that the way is open to manipulate one's own brain, or the brain of another, thus rendering both states of mind, and behaviour, malleable.

The social implications of all this are, of course, formidable to say the least. But then have not occultists, mystics and, worst of all, religious leaders, been working along these lines for centuries?

We are already aware of the fact that quantum effects can distort time, as may be evidenced in such psychic manifestations as clairvoyance, mental time travel, prophecy, etc., so, my main concern as relative to Carter's work is the effect of neural responses and machinations on the whole metaphysical arena. For example, Carter tells us:

> Religious belief and experience are usually regarded as beyond scientific exploration, yet neurologists at University of California, San Diego have located an area in the temporal lobe of the brain that appears to produce intense feelings of spiritual transcendence, combined with a sense of some mystical presence.

Canadian neuroscientist Michael Persinger, of Laurentian University, has even managed to produce such feelings in otherwise unreligious people by stimulating this area. According to Presinger:

> Typically people report a presence. One time we had a strobe light going and this individual saw Christ in the strobe ... [another] individual experienced God visiting her. Afterwards we looked at her EEG [electroencephalogram] and there was this classic spike and slow-wave seizure over the temporal lobe at the precise time of the experience - the other parts of the brain were normal.

Carter continues:

> The fact that we seem to have a religious hot-spot wired into our brains does not necessarily prove that the spiritual dimension is merely the product of a particular flurry of electrical activity. After all, if God exists, it figures He must have created us with some biological mechanism with which to apprehend Him. Nevertheless, it is easy to see that being able to get your God Experience from a well-placed electrode could - at the very least - undermine the precious status such states are accorded by many religions. How believers might cope with what many might see as a threat to their faith is one of the many interesting challenges that the brain will throw up in the coming millennium' *(Mapping The Mind,* pp. 18-19. Rita Carter, Weidenfeld and Nicholson, London, 1998).

Mapping the brain is nothing new, however, the first known brain-map having been found on an Egyptian papyrus which has been dated back as far as 3000 BC. Ancient Egyptian records confirm the knowledge of the hominid neural workings, probably gleaned from the practice of trepanning, for which there has been sufficient evidence to demand its acceptance by today's 'experts'.

To explain the full medical/mechanical details of the brain's workings demands the space of an entire book and, since my studies are more concerned with the effect of neural mechanisms from the metaphysical-cum-psychological standpoint, I would recommend those who might seek a more medical/anatomical approach to read Ms Carr's brilliant work, which can be easily understood by expert and layman alike.

The Role of the Brain in the Hominid Evolutionary Plan

A computer, as we know, is only as good as its software so, although our brains were obviously designed to accommodate the whole hominid evolutionary cycle, it would seem that appropriate software is only released to the human race as and when it is deemed necessary. In other words, human progress is 'regulated' from a higher source. So although the past has favoured us with a few great minds whose visions of the future have, sadly, often served to lead them to the heretic's pyre, the seeds they have sown have, in some subtle way, paved the path to that stimulation and understanding of the neural network destined to play its role in the next stage in the hominid development plan.

As I see and understand it, the brain contains the complete network for the whole hominid evolutionary programme, certain areas receiving 'external stimulus' at given times during the entire, pre-planned cycle. Looking back over the history of mankind as accepted by orthodoxy, the effect of some kind of evolutionary impetus is obvious; Primitive man, Neanderthal, Cro-Magnon - what next? The experts tell us that each of the aforementioned probably existed alongside the earlier prototype for some period. Now isn't this pattern beginning to assume the shape of a definitive blueprint, designed by some non-local force or superior mind?

Likewise, the evolutionary impetus is concerned with the albeit subconscious/unconscious effort to continually update the cerebral software, while also effecting a fuller, and more relatively appropriate use of the hardware available at any given period of time - in as many dimensions as the band-width of both the individual and overall field allow?

The work of Dr. John Gribbin alerted me to the role played by genes in this carefully constructed and divinely orchestrated evolutionary programme. The 'allele', for example, is a kind of 'sleeper gene' which appears to 'kick-in' and reprogramme the DNA to accept such phenomena as sudden and violent global changes. It has been rumoured that the century into which mankind has recently embarked is destined to be one of massive global upheaval - an axis tilt, perhaps, or even a pole shift, which phenomena could possibly expose all living things to new and lethal doses of solar radiation. My prophecy, for what it is worth, is that such an event has already been taken care of by neural/genetic pre-programming, as has always been the case in the past. Today's 'Neanderthals' will probably be confined to the pages of history and anthropology, along with the silicon computer, those destined to survive and create the 'new world' having been programmed to by-pass machinery and work direct from their own, neural computers. How will all this be achieved? By both the natural and educationally engendered expansion of the neural software. After all, Einstein, we are told, was not born a genius, he grew into one. His parietal lobe expanded as he studied maths (changed his software), the cranial output inevitably changing as certain areas of the brain are brought into prominence by one means or another. However, as far as intelligence is concerned, the close link between the genes and the brain has been highlighted earlier in this Chapter.

But are our brains really computers? All the evidence would seem to point in that direction. After all, the parasympathetic nervous system reacts in exactly the same way to an encounter with lightning as does a standard computer in that the outer casing is not affected but the software is, resulting in mental problems, loss of memory, and so forth. As someone commented recently, the brain could be likened to a termite mound in that the whole thing is larger than the sum of the parts.

In fact, the whole of creation can be viewed as a giant computer, programmed, perhaps, by a single mind or, more likely, by an infinite conglomerate of cells beyond the limited comprehension of mankind's present stage of evolution. We live in a dimension of time which represents a kind of sound-proof cage. We hear only our own voices and those sounds created at a level easily recognised by that area of the brain which computes both the identifiable and the enigmatic. And yet, since the hominid species first acquired a cognitive degree of consciousness (recognition?), there have always been those who have been able to penetrate this Time-barrier and converse with other sonic levels. Nuts, cranks or great spiritual leaders? Where is the dividing line? I am reminded of a true story which was also featured in a TV interview with the late Lord Soper. As 'Doctor Donald Soper', the worthy cleric, in his efforts to spread the gospel to as wide an audience as possible, was given to mounting a 'soap-box' at Hyde Park Corner in order to make his point. Needless to say he was more than often subjected to a considerable amount of heckling and, on one particular occasion, a man challenged him thus: 'Ere, mate, what proof have we got that you're not barmy?', which provoked the response, 'And what proof have I got that YOU are not barmy?' Whereupon his heckler placed his hand in his coat pocket and produced a sheet of paper which he waved triumphantly, 'Because I got me clearance from the asylum this morning, and 'ere's me certificate to prove it!'

I shall doubtless be labelled a 'metaphysical heretic' if I do not point the finger in the direction of those earlier-mentioned celestial programmers, who they are, and how they function. I can only refer to an earlier Chapter in which I have rendered a modicum of information on the kingdoms of Deva and how these operate in concert with evolution at all levels. In case you, the reader, feel that I have all, or even any of the answers to all this, I beg you to think again. There is a saying 'In the city of the blind the one-eyed man is king'. But as one who is devically partially-sighted, I can assure my readers - from first hand experience - that in the City of the Blind the one-eyed man is never a King but a heretic.

EPILOGUE

Daily Mail Literary critic, Jane Alexander, commenting on the latest book by James Redfield (of '*Celestine Prophecy*' fame'), on 4th February, 2000, effects an excellent critique on the works of this author in the following passages:

> *The Celestine Prophecy* became a worldwide bestseller, selling ten million copies in 35 countries. Frankly, the success of this spiritual adventure yarn was as mysterious as the event it described. The mystical 'insights' were mundane, the writing was execrable, the plot hung on by its fingernails ... so why is Redfield so popular ... Maybe the answer lies in his introduction. 'What we want is a life filled with mysterious coincidences and sudden intuitions that allude to a special path for ourselves in this existence'. (To which Ms. Alexander adds), Most people yearn for something beyond the mundane: the search for transcendence, for meaning, lies behind every religion and particularly the New Age crave for spirituality. However, modern seekers want it easy and want it now. No longer willing to trawl their way through spiritual classes or willing to meditate for hours, they want a quick-fix enlightenment. If it comes in the shape of simplistic lessons sugared by a page-turning plot, so much the better.

Bravo Ms. Alexander - for a while I thought I was the only one who viewed *The Celestine Prophecy* as a load of rubbish - a sort of fairytale for those adults who delight in the mysterious and transcendental. But then this is to be expected, psychological escapism from a harsh, materialistic world appearing to be one of the mental aberrations prominent in this age.

However, in the final analysis it will not be the fictional, romantic-type spirituality that will prevail after certain 'destined events' have taken place, but the essentially down-to-earth practicality that will be needed to establish both the new spiritual and empirical regimes that will eventually make their presence felt on this sad planet.

Although I am officially here in the 'observer' mode, it comes naturally to me to pass on at least some of what I, as a devic soul (field) have learned during my eons of experience, while also commenting on that which I see around me as viewed from an alien stance. It should be borne in mind, however, that in some matters, anyway, my perspective differs considerably from that of the average hominid, which naturally tends to render my viewpoint as vastly different from the stance assumed by the average seeker with whom I find myself in contact. It is for this reason that, in the aforegoing Chapters, I have sometimes had recourse to more orthodox schools of thought in order to make a point. Remember, I, too, am still but a student, and although I might appear to have a broader comprehension of other Universes and similar knowledge appropriate to my own kind, as far as the hominid experience is concerned I am still in the junior school.

One cannot expect a first-year student to understand and fully comprehend the kind of practical aptitude and overall information that he/she will encounter in more advanced classes. Even if one is an ardent 'swatter', keen to read well ahead of one's years (and designated school tutorials), unless such knowledge is placed into correct perspective by an appropriate tutor (be that one's own soul, some 'spiritual' preceptor, or experience pure and simple), it could be grossly misinterpreted and thus misunderstood. If you think about it, it has been clever brains that have invented instruments of war, destruction and suffering, which should serve as a salutary lesson to us all that no matter how high one scores on the MENSA tables, it is the soul-age that eventually decrees how, where and why we elect to employ such intellect as our genes have afforded us.

The whole of creation is 'ONE'. It is only in the lower echelons that it appears to be divided. But as these parts slowly evolve, they, too, will come to understand the true nature of that Whole, and in so doing, like many children who have eventually attained to adulthood, they will laugh at those 'spirituality' games that they played in their 'youth', and feel safe in the knowledge that at least one phase in their evolutionary tuition is done and finished with.

BIBLIOGRAPHY

Carter, Rita. *Mapping The Mind*, Weidenfeld & Nicolson, London, 1998.

Eysenck, Hans, & Sargent, C. *Explaining the Unexplained*, Weidenfeld & Nicholson, London, 1982.

Flaceliere, R. *Greek Oracles*, Elek Books, London, 1965.

Hope, Murry. *The Psychology of Healing*, Element Books, Shaftesbury, 1989.

Hope, Murry. *The Ancient Wisdom of Atlantis*, Harper Collins, 1995

Hope, Murry. *The Ancient Wisdom of the Celts*, Harper Collins 1995.

Hope, Murry. *The Ancient Wisdom of Egypt*, Harper Collins, 1995

Hope, Murry. *The Psychology of Ritual*, Element Books, Shaftesbury, 1988.

Hope, Murry. *The Way of Cartouche*, St.Martin's Press, New York, 1983.

Hope, Murry. *Olympus: An Experience in Self-Discovery*, Harper Collins, London, 1981.

Hope, Murry. *The Lion People*, Thoth Publications, Loughborough, 1988.

Hope, Murry. *The Paschats and the Crystal People*, Thoth Publications, 1992.

Hope, Murry. *The Gaia Dialogues*, Thoth Publications, Loughborough, 1995.

Hope, Murry. *Practical Techniques of Psychic Self-Defence*, Harper Collins, London, 1983.

Hope, Murry. *Practical Greek Magic*, Harper Collins, London, 1985.

Hope, Murry. *Cosmic Connections*, Thoth Publications, Loughborough, 1996.

Hope, Murry. *The Changeling* Light, Publishing for The College

of Psychic Studies, London, 1999.
Roney-Dougal, Serena. *Where Science and Magic Meet*, Element Books, 1991.
Mead, G.R.S. *Fragments of a Faith Forgotten*, John M. Watkins, London, 1931.
Sagan, C. *Cosmos*, Random House, New York, 1980.
Waite, A.E. *The Occult Sciences*, Kegan Paul, Trench, Trubner & Co.Ltd., London 1891.
Waite, A.E. *Alchemists Through the Ages*, Rudolph Steiner Publications, New York, 1970.
Walker, Barbara. *The Woman's Encyclopaedia of Myths and Secrets*, Harper & Row, San Francisco, 1983.

RECOMMENDED READING

The following is a list of relevant literature, some ancient, some more recent, which is grouped under appropriate headings:

Mediumship

Northage, Ivy. *Mediumship Made Simple*, Light Publications for the College of Psychic Studies, London, 1999.

General Magic/Occultism

Butler,W.E. *Apprenticed to Magic*, Thoth Publications, 2001.
Butler,W.E. *Magic Its Ritual, Power and Purpose*, Thoth Publications, 2001.
Butler, W.E. *The Magician - His Training and Work*, Thoth Publications, 2001.
Fielding,Charles & Collins,Carr. *The Story of Dion Fortune*, Thoth Publications, 1998.
Fortune,Dion & Knight,Gareth. *An Introduction to Ritual Magic*, Thoth Publications, 1997.
Fortune,Dion & Knight,Gareth. *The Circuit of Force*, Thoth Publications 1998.
Fortune,Dion. *Practical Occultism*, Thoth Publications, 2001.
Gray, William W. *Inner traditions of Magic*, Aquarian Press, London, 1970.
Green,Marian. *Practical Techniques of Modern Magic*, Thoth Publications 1993
Morrish, Furze. *The Ritual of Higher Magic*, Oak Tree Books.
Pennick,Nigel. *Practical Magic in the Northern Tradition*, Thoth Publications, 1994.
Richardson, Alan. *Priestess - The Life and Magic of Dion Fortune*, Aquarian Press, 1988.
Levi, Eliphas. *The History of Magic*, (Trans. A.E.Waite). Rider & Co., London, 1913.

Watson, Nancy B. *Practical Solitary Magic*, Samuel Weiser, Inc., Maine, USA, 1996). In your author's opinion this is the best occult primer available today. Not only does Ms. Watson know her occult, but she is also a competent psychologist.

Kabbalah/Qabalah

Butler, W.E. *Magic & The Qabalah*, Thoth Publications, 2000.
Denning,Melita & Phillips,Osbourne. *Entrance to the Magical Qabalah*, Thoth Publications 1997.
Fortune, Dion. *The Mystical Qabalah*, Ernest Benn, Ltd., London, 1935.
Knight,Gareth. *A Practical Guide to Qabalistic Symbolism*, Helios 1965.
Levi, Eliphas. *The Book of Splendours*, (Trans. A.E.Waite) Rider & Co., 1913.
Richardson, Alan. *An Introduction to the Mystical Qabalah*, Aquarian Press, London. 1974. Republished by Llewellyns (USA) as *Magical Gateways*. 1995.

Wicca/Witchcraft And Shamanism

Clifton, Chas. S. *Witchcraft Today*, Book Three - Witchcraft and Shamanism. Llewellyn Publications, USA. 1944.
Crowley, Dr. Vivianne. *Wicca, The Old Religion In The New Age*, Aquarian Press, 1989.
Drury, Nevill. *The Elements of Shamanism*, Element Books, Shaftesbury, 1989.
Green,Marian. *The Gentle Arts of Natural Magic*, Thoth Publications 1997.
Valiente, Doreen. *Witchcraft For Tomorrow*, Robert Hale, London, 1978.

Science

Braude, Stephen E. T*he Limits of Influence*, Methuen, 1986.
Gribbin, Dr.John. *In The Beginning - The Birth of the Living Universe*, Penguin Books Ltd., London, 1994.

Gribbin, Dr. John. *Timewarps*, J.M. Dent & Sons Ltd., London, 1979.
Hawking, Prof. Stephen W. *A Brief History of Time*, Hawking, Bantam Press, London, 1990.
Wolf, Fred Alan. *Parallel Universes*, Simon & Schuster, New York, 1988.
Zohar, Danah. *The Quantum Self*, Bloomsbury Pub. Ltd., London, 1990.

Other titles from Thoth Publications

THE LION PEOPLE
By Murry Hope

The author reveals her telepathic communications with the PASCHATS, a race of leonine beings from another world and another time.

DISCOVER:

* How all life relates to the Central Creative Force.
* The reality of other intelligent forms in the universe.
* The nature of death, karma and reincarnation.
* Why some people seem to have an easy life while others suffer.
* How to make time your friend not your enemy.
* A new concept of good and evil.
* Procedures of healing and self-healing.
* New and intriguing ways to self-discovery.
* The cosmic connection between Sirius and the planet Earth.

The author also provides evidence from historical sources, ancient arcane traditions, art, anthropology and astronomy, which lend credence to the existence of PASHATS and support for their message.

ISBN 1-870450-01-9

THE PASCHATS AND THE CRYSTAL PEOPLE
By Murry Hope

The sequel to *The Lion People*. Astounding revelations from another dimension of time and space, scientifically authenticated, covering - The impending Pole Shift; Cosmic genetic engineering?; The Quasi-crystal mystery; The cosmic virus that brought about the legendary 'Fall'; The role of animals on Earth; The role played by radioactivity in evolution; Science and the occult; and much, much more...

ISBN 1-870450-13-2